Interse[illegible] Stories

Narrative therapy reflections on gender, culture and justice

Edited by Dulwich Centre

ISBN 978-0-6481545-4-9

Dulwich Centre Publications
Hutt St PO Box 7192
Adelaide 5000, South Australia
Telephone +61 (8) 8223 3966
Email: dulwich@dulwichcentre.com.au
www.dulwichcentre.com.au

We would like to acknowledge the Kaurna people

who are the Traditional Custodians of the Land

on which Dulwich Centre stands.

We would like to pay respect to the Elders of the Kaurna Nation,

past, present and future, and extend that respect to other

Aboriginal Australians and Torres Strait Islanders,

to all the peoples who live on this beautiful land,

and to all those from many different cultures

who have made this book possible.

Contents

Setting the context

Feminisms, intersectionality and narrative practice

This book is the result of a *Feminisms, intersectionality and narrative practice* project at Dulwich Centre. This project hopes to engage with current trends in thinking and action in relation to gender diversity and intersectionality, and the challenges and opportunities these pose for the field of narrative practice. This project also hopes to address what seems to be an alarming fading of feminist consciousness within (some) narrative therapy professional circles. In the 1980s, feminist ideas transformed the family therapy world and were a key impetus in the development of what has become narrative therapy and community work. Now, 30 years on, it seems vital that intersectional feminist ideas are once again brought to the fore in shaping the future directions of narrative practice.

In the first phase of this project, practitioners from a wide range of contexts made short videos about why this feminisms and intersectionality project is relevant and important to them. These can be viewed at www.dulwichcentre.com.au/feminisms

The second phase of the project has involved the creation of a special position at Dulwich Centre: The Chair of Feminisms, Intersectionality and Narrative Practice. There are two current chairs, Tileah Drahm-Butler and Sekneh Hammoud-Beckett, both of whom have short pieces of writing included in these pages.

The third phase of the project involves the publication of these books:

- *Pathways beyond despair: Re-authoring lives of young people through narrative therapy* by Angel Yuen (2019)
- *Justice-doing at the intersections of power: Community work, therapy and supervision* by Vikki Reynolds (2019)
- and the book you have in your hands, *Intersecting stories: Narrative therapy reflections on gender, culture and justice*, featuring contributions by Tileah Drahm-Butler, Jill Faulkner, Alyssha Fooks, Sekneh Hammoud-Beckett, Renee Handsaker & Simangaliso Brenda Nyoni.

An upcoming book by Sekneh Hammoud-Beckett will focus on her sparkling narrative therapy practice with families that include young people of diverse sexualities, genders, cultures and religions.

Who knows what future directions this project will take, but let's continue the conversations!

I hope you enjoy the thoughtful and diverse contributions contained in these pages. This book would not have been possible without the hard work and astute, political, and graceful editorial skills of Claire Nettle. Kristina Lainson also played a very significant role in supporting the authors. Thank you Claire and Kristina and all contributors!

Warmly,
Cheryl White

Opening messages

Thank you

by Tileah Drahm-Butler

My name is Tileah Drahm-Butler.
I'm a Darumbal woman
who lives on beautiful Djabugay Country
in Kuranda, Far North Queensland.

I seek to always hold an
awareness of the country
and the peoples of the
land that I stand on
each time I speak,
and this is because,
as an Aboriginal woman,
I have been brought up knowing
the importance of history,
and of always honouring those
who have gone before us.

Women have
very much paved the way for me
and for the generations to come.

This includes the women in my family,
and also many other
women who I have not met,
and who my ancestors have not met.

I therefore am proudly feminist,
and I'm proud to bring my daughters up
with strong feminist values,
and to bring my son up
with these strong values too.

I'm lucky to be able to surround myself
with many strong women
who continue to fight in the many ways
for the rights of women.

I work in an emergency department
as a social worker in a hospital,
and each day
I see the many ways that gender shapes
our experience of the world.

Each time I work,
day or night,
I meet women who are affected by
violence perpetrated by men.

I also see how, in many ways,
the system continually fails to acknowledge that
this is a gendered issue.

I am constantly reminded
of the struggles that
are still ahead of us.

I also see
that the conversation is
continuing to head in the
direction that we need to go,
and this, of course, is thanks to
the constant voices of women.

One of the ways I seek to raise
the voices of women in my work
is through using narrative questions,
which centre the woman as
the expert on her life.

Whether this is through
providing an opportunity
to name the problem for themselves
through externalising questions,
or to name ways around the problem
through re-authoring questions.

Often, when I am having
these narrative yarns with women,
we end up talking about
the broader social context,
and the ways that patriarchy
is influencing our lives.

In these conversations,
we connect as women,
and this invites a balancing of power.
We can align ourselves as women
looking at the same problem
which is playing out
all around us.

This *Feminisms* project
is important to me
as we must keep the
voices of women strong.

I think that, in our society,
we are perhaps seeing a rise of bigotry.
Racism and patriarchy are
still certainly continuing.

And, therefore,
I remind myself
that I must continue to engage
in feminist movement
in any way possible,
to continue to strive for
social justice for all.

When we consider our experience,
and the experiences of the
people who we meet in our work,
within the context of
this intersectionality,
we still have so much to learn.

In particular,
I'm interested in learning about
the ways that I can join others in action.
This can be learnt from our history,
and through always keeping
the conversation happening.

For this,
I thank all those who are speaking
and all those who are listening.
All those who are writing
and all those who are reading
as part of this
Feminisms, intersectionality
and narrative practice project.

Thank you.

A letter to feminism

by Sekneh Hammoud-Beckett

I would like to acknowledge the Traditional Custodians of the Land on which I write. I would also like to pay my respect to Elders past, present and emerging. I bear witness to and honour their diversity, strength and resilience. As an Australian-Lebanese woman of Islamic heritage, I live on stolen land, a land that was never ceded, a land that belongs to Aboriginal people and Torres Strait Islanders. My work is in the context of a nation that was built on a history of genocide and the ongoing impact of colonisation.

I also pay my respect to people with diverse bodies, genders and relationships who continue to struggle in the pursuit of justice and who have created pathways for me to work.

I wish to also acknowledge Cheryl White, who introduced me to the different languages feminism speaks.

Dear Feminism,
Admittedly, my relationship with you has been mixed. Early in my career, I met your fundamentalist side. I was curtly advised that I could never truly embrace you because of my Arabic Muslim heritage and the way I presented myself in the world. I retorted that this strange stance sounded curiously similar to that of the patriarchs in my life.

Conversely, some Muslim leaders, colleagues and organisations were wary of you – they saw feminism as one of the insidious effects of colonisation. This was conveyed in language: there is no Arabic word for feminism, so the English word is used to describe you. However, the absence of a local name does not mean that people are not continuously advocating for women's rights in Muslim communities.

Quite honestly, it was a quagmire trying to understand your role across cultures. However, I think I have narrative therapy to thank for broadening my knowledge of your scope in people's lives.

I learnt my identities as a woman, and the people I am privileged to meet are constantly being shaped by competing Western and non-Western discourses. Narrative therapy allowed me to awaken from the effects of language-sleepwalking. It offered me landscapes in which to facilitate ongoing negotiations with you; to define myself and the possible identities that exist within each sociopolitical context. It provided a focus on researching people's creative acts of resistance – and people are not passive recipients of trauma, we often respond in accordance with what we give value to. Narrative therapy invited me to look beyond institutional knowledge and to research local wisdoms from women in my own backyard and over the fence.

Feminism, in your relationship with narrative therapy, you offered me the space to address patriarchy, sexism, racism, homophobia and transphobia in my own way, on my own terms, knowing full well we seldom escape the power structures that envelop our existence. The fact that I can write this letter to you tells me I am in a privileged space, treading pathways paved by significant people and a beneficiary of your role in all of our lives. The greatest knowledge I have gained in my relationship with you is that the less powerless we feel, the more significant this becomes in our lives.

With infinite gratitude,
Sek

Practice stories

Responding to women in prison who have used interpersonal violence:

a narrative approach disrupting binaries

by Jill Faulkner

I locate myself in the world as an intersectional feminist and prison abolitionist. I experience my life as having been shaped by multiple social locations including colonial settlement, both in my country of birth, Aotearoa, and in Australia on the lands of its First Nations peoples. Colonial settlement has produced accounts of women through patriarchal discourses that have shaped my and other women's experiences of interpersonal and systemic discrimination and abuse embodied in gender inequalities. Heteronormative narratives have othered LGBT, queer and nonbinary communities. Capitalism ensures that, like many other women, my future as I age remains less predictable, less sustainable. These social locations are not experienced as discrete accounts of my life, but as cumulative experiences over time that inform my participation in the world.

Many women in prison face multiple oppressions that intersect. They are experienced not singly but as a single synthesised experience (Crenshaw, 1991). Women who have been incarcerated have lived experiences of early abuse and trauma, poverty, violence as an adult and systemic racist discrimination. Prisons are not spaces of healing. Instead, they continue experiences of violence, abuse, subjugation and oppression. The prison–industrial complex appears to be the preferred approach to issues of poverty, homelessness, victimisation and systemic racism, continuing injustice for women, in particular Aboriginal women who are the fastest growing group of incarcerated people.

This chapter explores conversations I have shared with women in prison. These women have both used and been subjected to interpersonal violence. In this context, it has been important to find ways to make the operations of power visible. It is my contention that some of this power is concealed and contained in binary constructions of sex, gender, race and class, and that disrupting binary constructions makes it possible to reclaim the complexity of women's lives. It is my hope that these conversations can invite a shared interest in exploring a practice of examining, disrupting, shifting and dismantling the deep historical and structural systems of interlocking violence and oppression that are connected to interpersonal violence.

The following accounts of one-to-one and group work demonstrate my efforts to track the effects of power in naturalised binaries that are constituting of women's experiences. In these therapeutic conversations, I am alert to the ways social norms of gender produce interpersonal violence in women's lives. I am listening for how the labelling of women as 'perpetrators' is connected to the contexts of women's lives through experiences of sexism, poverty, race and class. For many women in prison, their offending is directly related to resisting the violence of men. Women's use of resistive violence challenges paternalistic notions of women as non-aggressive and shapes the criminal justice system's response to women who 'offend' gender norms (Sudbury, 2016, p. 17). Women with histories of early childhood violence and abuse often find that alcohol and drugs mediate the overwhelming emotional distress related to early abusive experiences. Naming these behaviours as effects of patriarchal violence and abuse provides possibilities for illuminating previously subordinated storylines. Enactments of violence in women's lives are linked to broader operations of social and state power. In drawing these links and working to disrupt binary ways of thinking, I invite women to see their own experiences as linked to a broader collective project that reveals violence as a social, rather than individual, issue (Denborough, 2013).

Women exiting prison

The work described in this chapter emerged through multiple conversations with women in the prison system. I was meeting with them because they had indicated that they wanted to 'get over' their trauma. This cohort of women has often been invisible to the human services system. Many manage the traumatic effects of their past experiences, and the dislocation involved in experiences of feeling invisible in their communities, by accessing hospital emergency departments or mental health services during crisis episodes. The women inevitably disengaged once the critical moment had passed, slipping into the shadows away from the social gaze. Women who have resisted or responded to violence in ways that do not fit with social notions of the 'good victim' are often redefined as the problem or misidentified as the perpetrator. As such, they are even less likely to receive assistance (Russo, 2019).

An element of my role was to link women, after their release, into a network of feminist services. The services I referred these women to are generally centre based and accessed through structured appointments. This arrangement did not enhance accessibility for this group: women exiting prison often become homeless and must deal with multiple requirements from community corrections to attend services and courses to prepare them to be 'good citizens'. This makes it difficult to get to appointments. Psychological discourses of 'client readiness' and requirements that 'complicating issues of drug use and mental health instability' be dealt with before the commencement of any 'therapeutic' work further inhibit access. These women and the conditions of their lives challenge notions of emotional and physical safety that trauma professionals often hold to be prerequisites for the work.

More broadly, the programs developed by community corrections and funded services to address the needs of people leaving prison are generally gender-neutral in approach and premised on notions of individual pathology, criminogenic behaviour and responsibility, with an intense focus on monitoring and changing the individual's behaviour, often under the guise of a trauma-informed approach. Research has consistently noted profound differences in the gendered experiences of female and male people who have offended (Steffensmeier & Allan, 1996, p. 460). Many women with experiences of incarceration live on the social and economic margins, struggling to survive and often engaging in a lifestyle that brings them into contact with the criminal justice system. Many have survived childhood sexual abuse, sexual assault and family violence. These experiences are often precursors to addiction, mental health issues and criminality. Many women report that their pathway into drug use, prostitution and crime began with running away in their early teenage years to escape family violence and sexual abuse. This early and continuing history of abuse often precipitates long-term physical and mental health problems (Covington, 2003). For many women, their criminalised behaviour represents multiple experiences of violation, abuse, subjugation and oppression by family members, partners and institutions including the police and the health care system. In my experience, women consistently speak about the absence of justice and healing for their herstories of harm, and this is reflected in research (Iman, Fullwood, & Paz, 2009).

In order to invite a hearing of the experiences of these women's lives, I provided a presentation to the Victorian Government at the invitation of the Inclusion and Diversity Unit of Family Safety Victoria. Women in prison requested that I incorporate the following points in order to illuminate some of their experience.

> 'Leaving prison is not easy'

The needs of women exiting prison are multimodal, and often their mental distress becomes more severe and crisis oriented on their release. Women exiting prison are often overwhelmed by the complexity of transitioning into the community.

> 'Without accommodation our choices are sex work or returning to violence or the drug dealer'

Most women exiting prison have two to four nights' accommodation in a motel and then need to present at homelessness services. Effectively, most women become homeless after their release. Many have relationships with drugs. Many have been responding to severe violence prior to incarceration and have comorbid presentations of mental health distress that often become more severe as they transition into unpredictability and poverty. The Victorian Royal Commission into Family Violence (2016, p. 239) found that 80% of women incarcerated in Victoria had histories of childhood abuse, sexual abuse, teenage and adult experiences of family violence with direct links to drug and alcohol use and offending behaviour. The royal commission acknowledged the absence of research findings on programs for women in prison who had 'perpetrated' violence (Victorian Royal Commission into Family Violence, 2016, p. 246). I was employed to implement programs for these women and to use these programs to build the research evidence.

Binary positions

The family violence sector, and related services such as the mental health and drug and alcohol systems, use the terms 'victim' and 'perpetrator' to position people affected by violence. This positioning is problematic in several ways. Violence is primarily an act – often a pattern of coercive and abusive acts – not a static, permanent identity or way of being

(Hyden, Gadd, & Wade, 2016). It also presents the categories of victim and perpetrator as distinct and mutually exclusive. When people have both used and been subject to interpersonal violence, the system is not structured to address this complexity. This necessitates 'an ongoing reflexive analysis of the multiplicity of individual identities and the interlocking nature of systems of privilege and oppression when disrupting simplistic, normative binary thinking' (Ristock, 2005, p. 68). The essentialist nature of binary descriptions of women's identities provides categories of identity that are totalising and often experienced as fixed, concealing an understanding of identity as multi-storied and a product of the ongoing negotiation of multiple subjectivities (Denborough, 2008). An integral part of social justice work is building the capacity to identify, question, interrupt and resist such binary thinking.

Binaries have a hierarchal structure in which the 'superior' term gets its superiority in direct relationship with the 'inferior' term. Male/female, white/non-white and victim/perpetrator are examples of this. Ravenscroft (2012) discussed how the race binary reinstates the superiority of the settler and coloniser through their naming of 'the Aboriginal' as inferior and giving no space for the naming of the settler self. The privilege contained in the capacity to name the 'other' is the privilege to create reality. This binary logic exponentially magnifies the power of the superior term (Crenshaw, 1991). The social construction of racial binaries establishes people who are classified white as educated, modern and in control of their own bodies, with the freedom to make their own decisions. People classified as non-white are established as inferior and are more likely to be associated with criminality (Russo, 2019). This structure of thinking has concrete effects. Currently, the greatest increasing cohort in prisons is Aboriginal women, who are generally serving remand in prison because they cannot meet the bail conditions for low-level crimes. People seen as deviating from the binary order can be subject to different forms of discrimination. Queerness and gender non-conformity are often conflated in the eyes of society with pathology and criminology (Russo, 2019). Violence against these groups is often minimised within criminal justice systems and the people themselves blamed (Merry, 2006). This is the violence of binaries.

Crenshaw (1991) noted that in the absence of noticing the way power circulates in these binaries, we fail to see how multiple layers of identity can amplify and complicate the experience of a problem. Patricia Hill Collins (1990) noted that lack of recognition of intersectionality leads to the erasure of people and their identities. Poststructuralist feminism places emphasis on the plurality of women's experiences and destabilises universal norms of womanhood (Russell & Carey, 2004). Many women in prison face multiple intersecting oppressions that are organised around structural, disciplinary, hegemonic and interpersonal domains of power. Binaries operate to keep structural inequities in place, one relying on the other to maintain the superior/inferior positionings. The power of the binary is that it becomes a lens through which we interpret ourselves and the world. Based in essentialist thinking, the dichotomised binary appears as a 'truth'; it is naturalised rather than recognised as having been made through culture.

Many women in the prison system are responding to multiple enactments of violence in their lives: interpersonal violence through families and partners; the violence of the state through the criminal justice system; the operations of systemic power that establishes the conditions for violence between women who are incarcerated; the violence of services in acts of regulation and exclusion; the violence of the medical system's pathologising of women's lives without consideration of the social conditions that shape them; the criminalisation of women who live in poverty; the violence of binaries that are produced through gendered, racialised and class-based ideologies (Allard, 2016). These multiple enactments of violence produced through an adherence to binary thinking are often experienced by women in terms of individual failure and responsibility. The rigid fixities of binaries locate problems within individuals, limiting possibilities for transforming oppressive and violent behaviours through recourse to the wider contexts that produce them.

In the conversations I hold with women in the prison system, I seek to map the effects of violence in their lives using tools from narrative practice to identify and disrupt binary thinking. I hope to open possibilities for women to experience alternative territories in their lives – territories that counter the multiple negative identity conclusions produced by these operations of power. The following is an example of this practice: the story of my meetings with Raelene.

Raelene

Raelene was an older woman who had found herself in prison for the first time. As frequently occurs, her crime had been reported in the media, which meant she had been subjected to a range of comments, questions and insults. Raelene had requested counselling to support her as she waited for the court to determine her sentence.

When Raelene and I met for the first time, we spent the first part of the session talking about ideas of safety and how we might structure safety in our conversations. Raelene said that she would not want to talk about certain times in her life, including what had happened to bring her to prison. She said she was more interested in talking about what was going on now so that she could 'get through' day to day. I asked her how she might let me know if any of my questions did not feel helpful. She responded that she would tell me that she didn't want to talk about those things. I suggested that navigating safety is something that we might see as an ongoing project that might change over time. Raelene agreed and spoke about having to think about safety in the compound, and how this changed depending on who was around. I asked about the effects of this vigilance. She responded that she had been well trained in 'watching over my shoulder'. I asked her what she would do if she were to support other women to manage their safety in the compound. Raelene responded with a range of skills that included: walking with your head up, finding safe spaces like the library where you could be busy and out of the way of gossip and prison politics, and learning to notice people's facial expressions because they could be an indication that care is needed, but also recognising that they might be about the person's inner world.

The collaborative process of structuring safety was a way of addressing relations of power within the therapeutic relationship and the different positions we each held in the prison system. If I stop noticing my power and privilege I may transgress. The idea that safety is not fixed but relational speaks to the dynamic construction of experience through complex interactions (Bird, 2004). It begins a second-story development founded on rich descriptions of skills and knowledges of 'being safe'.

Raelene was named in the prison system as an offender. In our first session together, I wanted to create the possibility of exploring other identity conclusions that would provide an alternative territory from which to explore the effects of the dominant story in future sessions. I was interested in beginning to understand the politics of the dominant story in Raelene's life. Holding a poststructuralist understanding of identity as multi-storied (Thomas, 2002), I was listening for dominant constructions of identity, and for ways this might relate to binaries that are shaped by hegemonic patriarchal understandings. I also wanted to listen for moments that might prove to be exceptions or sparks of resistance to this dominant story.

I asked Raelene what I might learn about her if I had a long time to get to know her. She responded with stories of her career and family, her passion for art and reading. She was delighted to hear that we shared many passions and that we had both worked in settings where people struggle against broader structures of oppression. She spoke about what she had been taught by the many different people she had supported. We shared laughter and a feeling of connection that was co-constructed in shared understandings of women's experiences. Women who have enacted interpersonal violence are often perceived as disrupting cultural representations of femininity (Yuen & White, 2007). In asking Raelene about what I might learn about her if I had months to get to know her, I was also exploring ways to contest binary notions of the feminine and of the perpetrator.

Raelene had been managing being in the prison environment by minding her own business, spending time in the library, taking care to eat as healthily as possible and walking all the time, doing many circuits of the compound during the day and evening. Recently, a person in her unit had threatened her because she often retired to her room after dinner to watch the news and this had been perceived as 'snooty and stuck up'. Raelene felt that she could hold her ground; however, the campaign against her increased with insinuations and loud threats about would be done to her when no-one was looking.

As I listened to Raelene describing her current problem, I noted that she cast herself in the role of 'perpetrator'. The assumptions that flow from this totalising categorisation had been active in shaping Raelene's identity in prison. Raelene said that she understood that she needed to 'earn' her right to be returned to the community one day: 'after all, I am a criminal'.

Raelene also disclosed that she had been having nightmares about times in her childhood. She would wake up in a sweat with her heart racing. She quietly wondered whether parts of her childhood that she had pushed away were making an appearance but said, 'today is not the day for remembering those things. I can't think about the distant past until I have been sentenced'. She also told me about a long-remembered dream about her affinity with birds in flight and how, when she felt troubled, she would imagine herself lifting off from the swamplands and gracefully riding the currents of the wind, out of reach. Transforming into a bird of flight in her mind had helped her flee early experiences of violence. I asked what she might call this practice of survivorship. She named it 'flights of fancy'.

The criminal justice system cannot solve problems of social inequality and oppression. Instead, prisons are sites where intersections of state violence and interpersonal violence, shaped by patriarchal norms, are internalised and played out (Hudson, 2006). I was interested in considering the sociopolitical context of the bullying Raelene had been experiencing. I asked what she had noticed about the ways that bullying behaviour liked to operate. She responded that she imagined that bullying had ideas about being 'better than others', being 'at the top of the pile' and being able to control others, and said that it was good at manipulating people. I asked Raelene what effect this bullying behaviour had on her. She reflected that it had separated her from others and brought embarrassment and feelings of shame. This had resulted in her feeling small and isolated in ways that she had experienced as a child. 'These feelings of smallness have been around forever', she said. I wondered aloud whether these ideas of domination and making people feel small and not good enough might be connected to ideas about superiority and domination that have been normalised in society. Raelene asked, 'are you talking about patriarchy?' I smiled and agreed, asking her what she knew about the effects of patriarchal ideas. Raelene responded that her father had used these ideas of superiority and men's ownership and control of women and children to hurt both her mother and her. She spoke about her father's idea that women amount to nothing, and how she had managed to finally escape this when she was 16 years old. She added that 'this is why I know so much about how to quietly find my way through'.

Raelene had spent many years 'finding the gaps' when her father was home. She took care that the younger children were 'out of his way'. I asked her whether there was anyone who would have noticed these acts of care for others. Raelene smiled and said a teacher had noticed her drawings of her siblings and invited her to Sunday lunches where she was able to read books and draw. This gave her respite from life at home. Raelene said that the teacher never mentioned knowing what was occurring in Raelene's family, but she would always give Raelene something to take home for her mother. I asked whether her teacher would be surprised to learn that Raelene had continued her commitment to caring for others and that she was still active in caring for women having hard times, even though this was frowned on by the corrections officers. Raelene replied that 'my teacher wouldn't be surprised, and in fact I made this my career'. We went on to talk about the other abilities and skills that Raelene had brought to her career. In this session Raelene had not wanted to talk about the abuses of her past. However, I was still able to draw out her skills and knowledges for surviving patriarchal violence. These skills had a long history and were embedded in skilful practices like embarking on 'flights of fancy', which she valued and practised often. I was drawn to her practices of care in what was at times a hostile environment. This spoke to the values and ethics that provided her with a foundation for living and for her work with others.

Sometime later, as an outcome of Raelene's initiative, we were able to spend more time together. She explained that she had been subjected to further bullying and harassment, including by the staff, and that she was looking for someone to remind her that she was 'sane' and not paranoid. The staff held institutional ideas that criminal behaviour was an individual pathology (Covington, 2003) and Raelene was fearful that the system wanted to make her mad because that would explain her criminal behaviour.

The following is a therapeutic document that I wrote to Raelene following this visit. The document provided an opportunity for additional witnessing of Raelene's preferred identity conclusions, which were in danger of being problematised and pathologised through the institutional gaze. The letter was designed to provide a portal into alternative storylines that at this point were barely visible to Raelene (see White, 2007).

> Dear Raelene,
>
> It was lovely to see you looking so well, albeit within the constraints that surround you, both seen and unseen! I have marvelled at your ingenuity in activating the system to be able to at least facilitate a further conversation between you and me – no mean feat! It had me thinking what an advantage it is to be a 'thin liner' for whom the ink and the rules are not so indelible and who can create space for manoeuvring! I am sure there is a long history of thin line activities that you have engaged in. I would love to know more about these and their history.

I have been feeling very honoured that you felt I would be able to stand with you against the multiple transgressions that have continued to occur. These enactments of power can be readily spotted by someone who has had to become well trained in responding to abuse – they require a survivor's eye. Unfortunately, others may minimise, conceal or down-play these acts and hand them back as if the responsibility belongs to those resisting violence within systems.

The idea that a football kicked at you is 'better than a smack in the ears' does not fit with safety and respectful relationships but is part of a patriarchal enactment of violence towards you as a woman. So easily it appears that when those in power are blind to these enactments, a woman's safety can be eroded. I don't believe that standing against this type of violence is being 'too sensitive'. When those in authority move towards protecting those who perpetrate violence against others in this way it leaves you 'having to be a bit plucky' for yourself. I am glad that your practices of being plucky for others are now being used to stand up for yourself. When taking a stand against these behaviours is translated as 'you seem to be holding on', an unspoken culture of forgetting these transgressions grows. It must have left you feeling quite alone when the corrections officer further excused this person's behaviour, saying 'what do you expect when we throw you lot all together?'

One of the knowledges that experiences of oppression and violence creates is a strong perception of threats to our safety. This means we are especially attuned to these violations. For many women for whom stories of pain and suffering shape their experiences in the world, things like strip searches or being forced to urinate in front of others can push us into spaces where feelings can become overwhelming, often carrying the intensity of early experiences. I am sorry that your refusal was not understood in the context of previous traumatic experiences. I am imagining that to then learn that refusal means you get written up as having produced a positive test must have felt like a further injustice. These ways of controlling others erode safety and trust in much the same way as other abuses in our lives.

I am reminded that you stated clearly to the officer: 'I am going now', and the response was: 'you are shouting at me'. How quickly things get elevated to the level of a transgression and then incur punishment such as taking your walks away. There are many unspoken messages in this treatment of you, which is aimed at controlling your behaviour and makes this 'a very dangerous place', as you described it.

I was deeply touched when you spoke about the medication that you are expected to take as part of your rehabilitation, and how you have continued to manage this on your own. I have a growing awareness of how much you have shouldered over many years as you have tried to protect people in your family, in your work and in the prison. Rather than seeing your refusal of the medication as defiance, it seems that your wisdom is standing alongside you, bringing an awareness of the possibility of becoming dependent on the medication. There are many knowledges and skills about recovery and punishment and what leads to a reparative and healing journey, and I wondered whether we might think together about ways to build on your innovations to bring ideas like trauma recovery to the people holding power in institutions. I wonder what knowing this might make possible for other women.

Travel well through your week.

Standing with you as a witness, respectfully,
Jill

Through this therapeutic letter, my intention was to make visible the enactments of violence that Raelene was responding to. Positioning myself as an ally, I was working to counteract the institution's pathologising of

Raelene's behaviour. In naming patriarchal violence and the tactics of violence against women embedded in behaviours of silencing and 'not noticing', I sought to ensure that Raelene was not positioned as the problem. I was aware that positions of power in the prison context impart not only a sense of the entitlement to objectify someone, but also a lack of consequences for those enacting harm. I wanted to address this as a social issue rather than allowing it to pass as an individualised problem that Raelene might internalise as evidence of not measuring up. My use of the term 'trauma recovery' was used cautiously. I am conscious that trauma is a term that conflates experiences of violation, oppression and subjugation and can invite people into a belief that the problem is in their brain via discourses of neuroscience and psychology. Raelene had shared that in prison it felt safer to speak of 'trauma' rather than of having been sexually abused as a child so I mirrored this language in the letter.

Raelene's efforts to humanise the prison continued as she resisted acts of violence against her. This disrupted identity constructions embedded in descriptions of women as passive and neutral, and assumptions about women as perpetrators. We were able to engage in what Denborough (2008) has described as considering the person as representing a social issue. For Raelene, this enabled her to feel connected to a collective endeavour to address women's experiences of violence in prison.

Reflecting on my conversations with Raelene and other women in prison, a recurrent theme has been the opening of space for women who have used interpersonal violence to be able to acknowledge and heal from violence, abuse and subjugations that they have been subjected to in the past. This is critical in moving towards a collective concern and commitment to refrain from using violence against others. It involves a rich description of the effects of the dominant narratives of women's lives, and deconstructing fixed and dichotomised identity conclusions produced through the violence of binaries. It involves identifying values, beliefs and commitments that support alternative stories that enable the women to acknowledge the harm they have done to others. This is made possible through offering experiences that allow an understanding of the self as socially constructed through broader social, political and cultural discourses. Women come to see their own and other's suffering as linked to power, control, poverty, racism and sexism, which interact with structures in society.

In my work with Raelene, consideration needed to be given to the violence that she had enacted. I have noticed in conversations with women in prison that because they have been identified as a 'perpetrator', and culturally women are trained to take responsibility, they readily speak about the harm they have caused. This has not been my experience in working with men who have used violence. Over time I have developed an approach in which I ask women if it's okay to hear more about their family, their siblings, the kind of things they did as a family, how school was for them and whether drugs or alcohol or violence had shaped their family life. Inevitably, stories of abuse are told. I then ask how these experiences shaped them as a teenager. I weave connections across time, listening for dominant, problem-saturated stories and for alternative storylines. This allows me to witness the injustice of women's lives as a foundation for later addressing the harm they have enacted. In these ways I seek to open landscapes of identity that are multi-storied and contest totalising constructions of women as 'perpetrators'. I also locate individual actions within broader operations of gendered violence, racism, classism and poverty.

From individual conversations to a group-work program

When I was contracted to respond to incarcerated women's use of interpersonal violence, I wanted to find ways to support women to renegotiate their relationships with anger and violence. A poststructuralist approach enabled me to stand aside from the idea that anger can be treated as a discrete identity that can be managed through taught skills. I was interested, instead, in bringing into view the complexities of women's lives, both historically and currently. In my work with women in prison, I have consistently heard women speak about their use of interpersonal violence in the context of past and current interpersonal violence. This complex relationship with violence is not acknowledged by services and disappears in the criminal justice system, with the law of provocation as a partial defence to murder having been abolished in Victoria in 2005. In many ways, I hoped that a program that attended to early experiences of violence and abuse might create possibilities for experiences of justice and being heard in ways that had not been present in women's lives. Denborough (2013) wrote of the possibilities for narrative approaches to address diverse concepts of justice. In considering narrative practices to resist binaries, I have been interested in the links between justice, healing and reparation. This, I believe, emerges out of a collective project of women sharing experiences (Hung & Denborough, 2013; Denborough, 2013).

Women's stories confirmed that their anger and use of violence was less likely to be driven by a sense of being entitled to harm and control another, as commonly characterises men's violence, and more likely to be used as a defence or resistance; an act of protection or anguish in the face of the abuse and violence they have been subjected to (Yuen & White, 2007). Experiences of responding to violence and harming others are not mutually exclusive. They are often an expression of what has been cherished and lost, which speaks to values and beliefs that open alternative storylines. The commonality of these experiences raised questions about how to approach work with women who have used interpersonal violence. I did not want to 'shut down' a form of anger that may have held legitimacy in the context of the women's lives – that may have been keeping them safe.

As I moved to extend the one-to-one conversations I had been having with women like Raelene into a new program of group work, I was alert to the possibilities of reproducing relations of power when working with women in prison. The co-facilitator of the group and I held a commitment to practicing in ways that are transformative of the social injustices inherent in the prison–industrial system, which is maintained through the creation of a culture of punishment and control (Fricker,

2007). Hare-Mustin (1994) argued that therapists are often engaged in activities of social control rather than effecting social change: therapy has the capacity to operate as a normalising activity. To avoid this possibility, we wanted to engage in practices of active listening in which the facilitators would not be at the centre. Such decentring practices can produce another kind of belonging: a belonging not conditioned on my own centrality (Russo, 2019).

Accountability

It was important that our commitment to transformative practices was held to account through an ethical framework and practices of collective responsibility (Reynolds, 2010). Hare-Mustin's (1994) work reminds us that both men and women participate in dominant discourses, including those relating to gender. bell hooks (2006) stated that no-one is exempt from the influence of patriarchy, which can be enacted by any of us. All too frequently, as Russo (2019, p. 1) stated, 'our praxis reproduces the power dynamics we are seeking to change'. To support me in bringing accountability to this work, I sought a community of practice that would meet regularly to build a culture of critique and hold extending conversations about the complexity of working with women who have used interpersonal violence and who have also been subjected to the violence, harm and subjugation of others. There were four members of the group, each with a different therapeutic orientation.

We used a series of questions to guide our conversations. These questions were influenced by questions posed by Aimee Carrillo Rowe in her book *Power Lines* (2008):

- When I'm speaking with someone who experiences structural oppression, in what ways might I perpetuate that oppression?

- How do I seek restorative action to redress the oppression I have enacted?

- What are some of the ideas produced by gender and racial binaries that I have grown up with?
- How do I disrupt the structures of binary thinking in which I have been raised?
- How are my own 'power lines' connected to structures of privilege and oppression?
- Whose wellbeing is essential to my own?
- Whose survival must be overlooked in order to connect to power in the ways that I do?
- How enmeshed am I in the systems we seek to change? For example, the carceral logic of guilt/innocence?
- As a practitioner speaking with women in prison, in what ways am I at risk of reproducing structural impositions of power?

The hope was that these ethical questions would support movement towards cultural humility in work with women in prison, and that the community of practice would provide an accountability structure that would hold my intentions for the work: to be generative of respect, knowing that power and privilege must be subjected to constant scrutiny in order to notice the struggles of others. These conversations continue as part of an 'imperfect project', and serve to hold me to account for my power and privilege in the work I undertake.

Inviting participation

My co-facilitators and I invited women interested in a program addressing women's use of interpersonal violence to join us in a focus group to be held in the prison. Eighteen women attended. The questions we were to discuss were subjected to the gaze of the Department of Justice, which articulated some key elements that we were to treat as essential to the delivery of programs for 'perpetrators': 'perpetrators' must be held accountable and kept in view at all times' and 'collusion with perpetrators is not to be tolerated'. Keeping these directives in mind, we planned and guided our exploratory focus group conversation.

Before putting questions to the group, we presented the following explanation of the purpose of our meeting:

> We understand that over 80% of women in prison were harmed as children or suffered partner and family violence as adults, and that these experiences often lead to behaviours that harm both ourselves and others.
>
> Groups for women who have used violence have not been run in many places in the world. We want to work together to make sure we shape the group we are planning in ways that are helpful, healing and support you in gaining skills to manage your lives. It is important to us that those who join the group become co-researchers so that we can find out what works and pass this knowledge on to others. In many ways you will be shaping the path not only for new possibilities in your future but for many other women and, importantly, all our children.
>
> Some of the questions we ask may not be relevant to you personally, but we encourage you to think about other people you know and to share your thoughts and ideas.

After this preamble, we posed a series of questions:

- When you were growing up, what were the ideas in your family about gender?
- What do you think these ideas made possible for you and how did these ideas limit you?
- What is the most important role you have in the world? What would help you or support you to fulfil this role in the way you want to?
- When you think about the kind of person you want to be in the world, how is this different to who you are now and what do you feel needs to change?

- If you think about times when you've acted in ways that have harmed others, what would be helpful to understand or know more about so that you can do things differently in the future?
- Is there past hurt that constantly sabotages or gets in the way of who you want to be in the world?
- What might you want to know more about to make your hopes and dreams for a different life on your release come true?

Some of the ensuing discussion was captured in a therapeutic letter to those who participated. It was read to the women three weeks later in the first session of our group-work series. All the women who had attended the focus group chose to participate.

> To each of you who attended the focus group,
> I want to thank you for the care and thought you brought to our meeting. These were hard questions and I was touched by the way you looked out for other women in your responses, checking to make sure that everyone's voice was heard. I wondered about how you had found ways to hold on to these practices of respect in prison, where the value of making space for everyone's voice is not so alive.
>
> Many of you spoke of wanting to learn more about your anger, and there were stories about how anger had taken hold of your lives in ways that both terrorised you and had you terrified of the harm that you could do. I wondered what your concern about this said about each of you and what is important to you in moving forward in your life. It had me thinking about values of wanting to do no harm, a position against violence. I look forward to hearing more of your ideas about this.
>
> Since our conversation, I have been thinking about anger and how it can lead to the use of violence. I wondered what might be made possible if, as a group, we were to explore the times when

anger is most often around, and what anger might tell us if it had a voice. Many women have spoken to me about how their anger has become a flag that something is unfair or unjust. I heard you speak about how anger had led to ways of controlling others. I also heard ethics of care and responsibility. I would like for us to more richly explore these in our time together.

I heard many of you speak about your yearning for belonging and reconnection with families and children, and a desire to learn more about how you might do this in different ways – how you might live lives with 'more respect' and 'make good' the harm you have caused. These sentiments struck me as standing for responsibility. I have been thinking about what others in your families might say if they could hear about these commitments and the hopes that you are holding as you begin working with this group.

It was an emotional conversation in which many spoke about what they had learnt about being a woman in their family. There were stories of hardship and painful experiences, including abuse by fathers, brothers and uncles. I heard that, for many, these experiences were accompanied by memories of feeling disconnected, alone and angry. I am sorry that, for so many, suffering shaped your lives as children. I am interested in learning more about your skills of survival in hard and abusive times. I have been thinking about what these skills might make possible for your journey in this program, in which we will look at the stories of your past and address both your own healing and the pain and hurt that we have caused others. I am imagining that as your knowledges are shared in the group, they will become a powerful resource for each of us.

A program for women who have used interpersonal violence is a new undertaking for us. I have been holding an idea that you might think about being a co-researcher with us as we run the program, helping us to ensure that the program is travelling in ways that are helpful to each of you, and that we are speaking in ways that are meaningful and support a journey that fits with your values and hopes for your future.

In these ways we will be creating a path for other women.

Warmly,
Jill

The women were excited about the idea of joining us as co-researchers in developing our understanding of the experiences of women in prison. Bird (2004) described the search for an explanation whenever something in our lives goes wrong. People with histories of traumatic violence and abuse can end this search with an unresolvable conclusion that they are bad. Such life-defining 'truths' gather strength whenever they are confirmed in several locations, such as family and significant societal institutions. Responses that echoed this pattern shaped our ideas about the group, prompting a focus on co-creating different landscapes of identity before inviting stories about hurt and pain.

Within the constraints of the prison–industrial complex, opportunities were set up to gather the women's thoughts on the challenges they encountered in the group learnings and on what could be done differently. This included setting up a postbox in which women could anonymously leave comments during or after sessions, and a canvas that collected pictures and comments about what had caught participants' attention during the program. At the end of each group meeting, we invited reflection on the ideas and activities that the women had enjoyed, and any they felt needed to be changed. Each woman also attended a one-to-one session, during which her comments on the program were elicited. A focus group with an external evaluator was a further opportunity to capture the women's thoughts about their experience of the group, and about what worked well and what might be changed.

Conclusion

In working to address women's use of violence, I have been struck by the injustice of the serious harms done to women, and how recognising the absence of this narrative in women's use of interpersonal violence offers a starting point to disrupt binary positions of perpetrator/victim. These conversations support women to notice the effects of sexism and patriarchal ideas that are informed by the gender binary, and enable the naming of ways in which women have responded to or resisted such effects. I name the operations of power in ways that support people like Raelene to feel 'sane'. As women notice the effects of these ideas in their lives, and how they produce and legitimise men's entitlement to use violence and abuse in the subjugation of women and children, further stories of resistance and survival become available. Connecting small acts of resistance to a broader story of injustice becomes possible through exploration of ways people have been harmed and how they have responded to and resisted violence and abuse. Tracking women's resistance enables meaning to be made of their behaviour in ways that contest binary notions of female passivity. We see actions that are consistent with people's values and commitments for their lives. Importantly, we understand that people are always seeking safety (Reynolds, 2010). Documenting women's resistance supports them to move from binary notions of individual deficit to locating their experiences within patriarchal structures as a social issue.

Acknowledgment

I want to express my heartfelt respect for the women who continue to find ways to resist the overwhelm of a system that has failed to provide care and justice.

References

Allard, P. (2016). Crime, punishment, and economic violence. In INCITE! Women of Colour Against Violence (Eds.), *The colour of violence* (pp. 157–163). Durham, NC: Duke University Press.

Bird, J. (2004). *Talk that sings: Therapy in a new linguistic key*. Auckland, New Zealand: Edge.

Collins, P. H. (1990). *Black feminist thought, knowledge, consciousness and the politics of empowerment.* Boston, MA: Hyman.

Covington, S. (2003). A woman's journey home: Challenges for female offenders. In J. Travis & M. Waul (Eds.), *Prisoners once removed: The impact of incarceration and re-entry on children, families and communities* (pp. 67–104). Washington, DC: Urban Institute.

Crenshaw, K. (1991). Mapping the margins: Intersectionality, identity, politics and violence against women of colour. *Stanford Law Review, 43*(6), 1241–1299.

Denborough, D. (2008). *Collective narrative practice. Responding to individuals, groups and communities who have experienced trauma*. Adelaide, Australia: Dulwich Centre Publications.

Denborough, D. (2013). Healing and justice together: Searching for narrative justice. *International Journal of Narrative Therapy and Community Work*, (3), 13–17.

Fricker, M. (2007). *Epistemic injustice: Power and the ethics of knowing*. Oxford, England: Oxford University Press.

Hare-Mustin, R. (1994). Discourses in the mirrored room: A postmodern analysis of therapy. *Family Process*, (33), 19–35.

hooks, b. (2006). *Outlaw culture: Resisting representations*. New York, NY: Routledge.

Hudson, B. (2006). Punishing monsters, judging aliens. *Justice at the Borders of Community,* (3), 232–247.

Hung, S., Denborough, S., & Denborough, D. (2013). Unearthing new concepts of justice. *International Journal of Narrative Therapy and Community Work*, (3), 18–27.

Hyden, M., Gadd, D., & Wade, A. (2016). Introduction to response based approaches to the study of interpersonal violence. In M. Hyden, D. Gadd, & A. Wade (Eds.), *Response based approaches to the study of interpersonal violence* (pp. 1–16). New York, NY: Palgrave McMillan.

Iman, J., Fullwood, C., & Paz, N. (2009). *Girls do what they have to do to survive: A study of resilience and resistance.* Chicago, IL: NSWP Global Network Sex Work Projects.

Merry, S. E. (2006). *Human rights and gender violence: Translating international law into local justice*. Chicago, IL: University of Chicago Press.

Ravenscroft, A. (2012). *The postcolonial eye: White Australian desire and the visual field of race*. Farnham, England: Ashgate.

Reynolds, V. (2010). A supervision of solidarity. *Canadian Journal of Counselling, 44*(3), 246–257.

Ristock, J. (2005). Taking off the gender lens in women studies: Queering violence against women. *Canadian Women's Studies, 24*(2/3), 65–69.

Rowe, A. C. (2008). *Power lines: On the subject of feminist alliances*. Durham, NC: Duke University Press.

Royal Commission into Family Violence. (2016). *Final report of the Royal Commission into Family Violence*. Melbourne, Australia: Victorian Government Printer.

Russell, S., & Carey, M. (2004). *Narrative therapy: Responding to your questions*. Adelaide, Australia: Dulwich Centre Publications.

Russo, A. (2019). *Feminist accountability: Disrupting violence and transforming power*. New York: New York University Press.

Steffensmeier, D., & Allan, E. (1996). Gender and crime: Towards a gendered theory of female offending. *Annual Review of Sociology, 22*, 459–487.

Sudbury, J. (2016). Rethinking anti-violence strategies: Lessons from the Black Women's Movement in Britain. In INCITE! Women of Colour Against Violence (Eds.), *The colour of violence* (pp. 13–24). Durham, NC: Duke University Press.

Thomas, L. (2002). Poststructuralism and therapy: What is it all about? *International Journal of Narrative Therapy and Community Work*, (2), 85–90.

White, M. (2007). *Maps of narrative practice*. New York, NY: Norton.

Yuen, A., & White, C. (Eds.). (2007). *Conversations about gender, culture and narrative practice: Stories of hope*. Adelaide, Australia: Dulwich Centre Publications.

Intersectional conversations:

Talking about racism and white privilege with counsellors working in sexual assault and family violence

Alyssha Mary Fooks and Simangaliso Brenda Nyoni

> Everyone has a voice but not everyone gets given equal opportunity to use it. In the project described in this chapter, I expressed my voice and my experiences without fear. To all counsellors of colour and Aboriginal counsellors, this chapter is in your honour. To all the white counsellors out there who are working to be aware of privilege and make it their utmost priority to acknowledge white privilege and call out racism, I honour you too. To the white counsellors who can tolerate being uncomfortable and yet boldly have these conversations, thank you for walking with us. – Simangaliso Brenda Nyoni

Introduction and background

Ethnicity, race and culture are essential considerations in the work of responding to sexual assault and family violence (Ridgeway, 2015). There is growing acknowledgment of the impacts of racism on our health, wellbeing and safety (Australian Human Rights Commission, 2019).

People and communities of colour and Aboriginal people have extensively described the impacts of racism across their lives (Blair, Dunn, Kamp, & Alam, 2017; Ridler, 2018). Racism operates in counselling settings too, but it is often hard to name and address. There are times when race and racism are rendered invisible by whiteness (Frankenberg, 1993) and the dominance of white privilege.

Using a narrative therapy framework, we set out to spark conversations about racism and white privilege in organisations that respond to family and domestic violence and to sexual assault. This became a collaborative project that sought, first, to elicit rich descriptions of the skills and knowledges of Aboriginal women and women of colour working to support victim-survivors of sexual assault and family violence. Second, influenced by the work of Moreton-Robinson (2000), we sought to interrogate white privilege through engaging in conversations with white women working in the sector, inviting them to step up to address their own privilege and to foster practices of accountability.

The work described in this chapter strives to credit and honour the experience of Aboriginal people and people of colour. In the words of Aunty Barbara Wingard and Jane Lester (2001), we have sought to support people in 'telling our stories in ways that make us stronger', acknowledging that 'our stories are precious' (2001, p. 1).

This chapter does not detail the work of providing counselling within a narrative or antiracist framework. Nor does it suggest how to work cross-culturally or with cultural safety. Instead, it focuses on the experience of inviting conversations about racism, white privilege and intersectionality (see Crenshaw, 1989) as they operate in the work contexts of therapists and counsellors. We involved Aboriginal women, women of colour and white women from a diverse range of settings: health agencies, private practice, sexual assault and family violence counselling, education and prevention of violence work. This chapter describes the questions we developed to prompt these sometimes uncomfortable conversations, some of the ethical dilemmas we encountered and what we learnt about talking about race, racism and white privilege.

How the project came about

The work described in this chapter was a collaboration between Simangaliso and Alyssha, who met working together in a sexual violence response service. Simangaliso is a black/African woman who works as a counsellor and advocate. Alyssha is a white, queer, cisgender woman who works as a social worker and facilitator-supervisor. The work began with the brief but compelling conversation that ensued when Alyssha took the necessary and important step of asking Simangaliso whether she had experienced racism in her workplaces. The answer was yes.

Simangaliso shared some of the effects of racism and white privilege on the way she functioned as a human being and as an African counsellor, including subtle and undermining experiences like the frequency with which people questioned her qualifications or brought attention to her African background. Simangaliso shared an experience of working with an Aboriginal woman who had expressed joy and relief that she had been allocated a black counsellor. However, sometimes clients of the service asked not to work with her, which she knew was about her being African. These experiences could be isolating and difficult to talk about. Simangaliso emphasised the importance of talking about racism, and imagined creating a space where people of colour and white people could talk openly and comfortably about race, racism and privilege.

We decided to try to create such a space for conversation about racism and white privilege, and to consider the ways in which these forces are present in work with survivors of sexual and family violence. Would women of colour in our networks like to talk about some of the things we were grappling with? Were Simangaliso's experiences mirrored in other women's experiences? How were white colleagues addressing issues of power and privilege? We set out to explore the intersectional knowledges of our own professional colleagues, and to learn from other women of colour and Aboriginal women who were involved in sexual and family violence work.

Our informal conversations evolved into a project in which Alyssha and Simangaliso collaborated in co-research. Simangaliso brought expertise in intersectionality in counselling and acted as a consultant to the interview process and the writing of a collective document. Alyssha developed ways to use narrative practices to further the project, taking responsibility for conducting interviews and interrogating white privilege and power.

Designing for accountability and partnership

As someone who benefits from white privilege and holds power in her work roles, Alyssha was concerned about the potential to impose oppressive research on marginalised and oppressed communities (Chilisa, 2012; VicHealth Koori Research and Community Development, 2000). She questioned whether it was her role to introduce conversations about race and racism, or to document the stories and skills of women of colour. Would this risk further marginalising the stories and experiences of women of colour and Aboriginal women? The Just Therapy Team of Aotearoa New Zealand described how:

> … many people in this situation feel overwhelmed with the enormous process of changing the institution they work in, afraid of the bewildering implications for their own future and the possibility they might cause the same offence sometime in the future. To avoid these risks and open conflict, they do nothing and feel impotent. Unfortunately, the passivity functions as a form of control because it further entrenches the status quo. (Waldegrave, Tamasese, Tuhaka, & Campbell, 2003, p. 4)

Although white privilege encouraged and allowed Alyssha to remain silent as her colleagues grappled with the injustice of racism and oppression, Alyssha decided not to submit to the resigned passivity that the Just Therapy Team described. Concluding that if she did not do this work, she would be giving white privilege free space and power, she sought support and guidance from courageous women of colour who she knew would provide honest and direct feedback. Their response was enthusiastic, and they expressed relief that the importance of conversations about racism and white privilege was being acknowledged and that someone else was taking on the labour of raising these issues. Alyssha arranged external supervision from narrative practitioners Sekneh Hammoud-Beckett and Tracy Castelino to provide further accountability and partnership. 'Partnerships of accountability … facilitate the responsibility of dominant groups to deconstruct their dominance' (Waldegrave et al., 2003, p. 101). Partnerships have also been important within narrative therapy (Denborough, 2012; M. White, 2003) as these contribute to shaping the stories and experiences of our lives. The partnership between Alyssha and Simangaliso was crucial to this work. Our regular and robust conversations created the conditions for Simangaliso's knowledge and experience as a black African woman to significantly inform the focus of our questions and the ways the collective document was shared.

Racism in the sexual assault and family and domestic violence sectors

In Australia, violence against women and children is now widely recognised as a serious and preventable problem with enormous individual, community and social impacts (Our Watch, 2018; Vic Health, 2019). The struggles and activism of Aboriginal, white and women of colour feminists have brought attention to this issue and have led to the establishment of services that respond to violence and harm.

The mainstream Australian sexual assault and family violence sectors arose directly out of feminist activism that occurred during the 1970s and 1980s. Feminists have long linked sexual assault and violence against women to the broader social and political impact of men's power and entitlement over women and children. Through the work of feminist women and their allies, sexual assault services were created. The government-funded support services that exist today grew out of pioneering crisis response services managed by unfunded feminist collectives (Hewitt & Worth, 2014). However, 'these early women's liberation conversations were very Euro-centric. When talking about "women's experiences" we were overwhelmingly referring only to white women' (C. White, 2016, p. 10). The particular needs of women of colour and Aboriginal women were rarely considered. Because mainstream services were and are not always accessible or culturally responsive to Aboriginal women and women of colour, new organisations were established to counter the impacts of white privilege. These were led and staffed by Aboriginal women and women of colour. Examples include the Centre for Multicultural Women's Health, established in 1978; Intouch, established in 1984; and Djirra, established in 2002. Despite the advocacy of these organisations, racism and white privilege still hold power in the sexual assault and family violence sectors.

Some feminist frameworks for responding to sexual assault have failed to attend adequately to the implications of race, culture, ethnicity and migration on the experiences of people seeking services relating to sexual assault or on the practitioners providing care. Although some agencies have made attempts to become more responsive to and inclusive of the needs of women from diverse backgrounds, this isn't always taken up as an organisational priority. A consultant to this project shared her observation that the need to improve responsiveness to clients' diverse cultural needs, and to address the lack of diversity in sector staff, was frequently identified during planning processes, but that these were not pursued, instead being continually relegated to the 'back burner'.

Planning our initial research conversations

Our first research conversations were with Aboriginal women and women of colour who were in our professional networks. They built on the informal conversations that Alyssha, Simangaliso and others had been having, and included reference to some of the shared experiences we had already identified. We developed a series of questions to document experiences of racism and to highlight participants' values, knowledge, agency and resistance (M. White & Epston, 1990), including skills in working with clients of diverse cultural backgrounds. Cultural knowledges have not been seen to be significant in clinical work (Waldegrave et al., 2003). With these questions we hoped to create a space that would welcome and celebrate the unique skills and cultural knowledges of Aboriginal women and women of colour:

- Why have you decided to share your story with me today?
- What does your reason for deciding to talk about the effects of racism in your work say about what is important to you?
- Has anyone informed these values?
- What skills and knowledges do you hold as a woman of colour doing this work?
- Can you share a story from your counselling practice that you think went well, or that you really learnt something from, and that you think might be helpful for other women of colour counsellors and/or for counsellors with white privilege?
- What skills and knowledge did you draw on for this to go well? Where did those skills, that knowledge, come from? Where did you learn these? From whom?
- As a counsellor or when delivering training, do you get asked questions about your qualifications?
- Do you get asked about your cultural background by clients? What are some of the effects of these questions and how do you respond?
- Is creating a space to talk about racism of interest to you?
- What are the conditions or contexts that enable you or others to talk about race, racism or privilege at work?
- If you were to talk about working as a woman of colour at your agency, what would be most important for you to share?

- Are there times that race has been either highly visible or rendered invisible in work with clients or in your team?
- What parts of your agency model or intake process do you use when working with women of colour? Thinking about the feminist model, are there ways that you change your discussions with different clients?
- If you were to think about your agency's frameworks and models or codes of practice, do they resonate with culturally and linguistically diverse clients?
- Are there ways that you do things differently when you are consulting with women of colour? Can you tell a story about this?
- Is there anything that you would like to add to what we have discussed?

We began by trialling these questions with Alyssha interviewing Simangaliso, and then in conversations with five of the women from our networks who had generously agreed to participate. These conversations were recorded and later transcribed.

In addition to informing the list of questions that were our starting point for the interviews, narrative ideas guided our stance of being decentred and influential, and valuing people as experts in their own lives (Morgan, 2000). During the interviews, Alyssha used narrative practices including externalising problems, mapping the effects of problems, re-authoring, identifying unique outcomes and documenting alternative storylines (M. White, 2007).

marcelo polanco (2013) demands that narrative therapists consider how our therapeutic work can avoid becoming another site of colonisation. Decolonisation (Chilisa, 2012; Land, 2015; Sherwood & Edwards, 2006; Tuhiwai Smith, 2012) was an important consideration for moving into this work. Aboriginal nursing academics Juanita Sherwood and Tahnia Edwards (2006) have written that 'decolonising processes require individuals to explore their own assumptions and beliefs so that they can be open to other ways of knowing, being, and doing' (2006, p. 188). The conduct of the interviews was also informed by the decolonising interview principles outlined in *Indigenous research methodologies* (Chilisa, 2012), in particular, the idea that an interview is a ceremony. This required that we create space and time for an interview to occur, give voice to participants, share about ourselves as interviewers and communicate interest in the conversations. During the conversations, Alyssha focused on maintaining a posture of collaboration and partnership – checking in, using questions like 'How is this conversation for you?' and creating space for people to direct our conversations by asking, 'Should we keep talking about … or would you be more interested in speaking to something else?' Questions were asked with genuine curiosity and openness. Alyssha paid vigilant attention to the potential biases and privileges she carries as a white woman, knowing that these would be present and trying to mitigate their effects by maintaining a position of curiosity and avoiding making assumptions (Morgan, 2000). Dominant discourses of white privilege were ever present during the interviews.

An important consideration was the structuring of safety in this process. This was informed by Simangaliso's expertise and by the work of Reynolds and Richardson/Kianewesquao (2014). One participant suggested that safety was created for her by 'being part of a larger collective conversation'. After the initial interviews, Alyssha recognised that she needed to create space for people to decline to answer questions. We added into the conversations a question from Reynolds and Richardson/Kianewesquao: 'What will it take for you to say no to me if I ask a question that is not right?' (2014, p. 154). To this we added '… or that you do not want to answer?' These questions created space to explore how people wished to engage in the conversations and were important in the subsequent interviews.

Introducing re-membering practices

In addition to the questions above, re-membering practices were used to make visible the skills and knowledges of the counsellors. Re-membering practices were introduced to narrative therapy by Michael White (2007), who drew on the work of anthropologist Barbara Myerhoff. Myerhoff identified the significance of attending to 'the figures who belong to one's life story' (Myerhoff, 1982, p. 111). Re-membering practices have been described as:

> … holding particular people in one's heart and mind as a personal team, and owning their experiences of oneself, [which] allows people to know themselves in a community of choice, rather than one of chance. This can make all the difference. (Russell & Carey, 2004, p. 55)

Re-membering practices enabled us to further conversations about the counsellors' values, skills and knowledges through exploring the people and relationships that supported them.

The contribution of re-membering practices to our interviews can be seen in the following extract of Alyssha's interview with Simangaliso. Simangaliso had mentioned her grandfather and his home, where they lived together in Zimbabwe. Alyssha sought to bring forward this relationship as a way of re-membering and honouring his contributions as an encouraging and supportive person in Simangaliso's life, and to invite rich description of Simangaliso's work and life.

Simangaliso had spoken about challenging white privilege, which she described as the 'courage to say the unspoken' and to have 'difficult conversations'. At this point, Alyssha asked re-membering questions that invited Simangaliso to link her life with her grandfather's life through their shared purposes. In the face of the isolating effects of racism, Alyssha hoped that this line of questioning might contribute to an alternative story of connection.

Alyssha: Has anyone informed these values that you describe? Who comes to mind?

Simangaliso: My grandfather has always been the biggest influence on everything I choose to do. His teachings, words of advice, and his role within his family and community have been the things I draw mostly on in what I value and I am committed to my work. He believed in never doing something half-heartedly as he believed this to be a missed opportunity to affect others, to grow as a person and to network. He didn't believe in coincidence but purpose and a reason for everything and that it was up to an individual to decide what meaning they made of their life experiences.

Alyssha asked Simangaliso if she would be interested in talking more about her grandfather.

Alyssha: Would he be surprised by your commitment to this work?

Simangaliso: My grandfather wouldn't be surprised at all.

Alyssha: If I were to ask your grandfather about your 'courage to say the unspoken', what might he share with us now?

Simangaliso: He would have a smirk on his face and say, 'I have always known she would become this'. He had such faith in me and my ability to be and achieve anything. My grandfather was the first child from a father who had three wives. He was considered the head of the family. I grew up watching him having difficult conversations with different people, and noticing his ability to command himself in any situation. He modelled what he wanted me to aspire to be: a conqueror and a fearless woman.

Alyssha: What is it that your grandfather knew about you, or that he might have witnessed you doing, that would have told him that courage to say the unspoken was important to you?

Simangaliso: My grandfather attended many of my public speaking events. He would sit in the front row with such pride. This gave me courage, always, and helped ease public speaking jitters. He was always so present during my presentations. The fact that I was never scared to speak in a public forum for him meant I could speak about anything to anyone.

Alyssha: What might your courage to say the unspoken have contributed to his life?

Simangaliso: It gave him joy – a second chance to parent but this time with less pressure because I was his grandchild not his child.

Through introducing re-membering practices in our interviews, we were able to honour and bring forward the skills and knowledges of workers of colour, the social histories of these skills and knowledges, and also stories of people, like Simangaliso's grandfather, whose legacy continues to inform people's lives and work.

> I've never known this linking not to be important. These questions ask people to provide a two-way account of relationships, they make visible the contribution of people in each other's lives and, when we are especially lucky, along with all that, they reinvigorate relationships. These events go a long way in supporting people's preferred experiences of life. (Freedman, 2011, p.5)

The intention was to invite Simangaliso to consider how the actions and commitments she described might be important, not just for her, but for her grandfather as well. This was a bringing forward of this relationship to support preferred stories of identity.

Inviting difficult conversations

After reflecting on the initial interviews, we sought to invite further conversations about the unique skills and knowledges that other women of colour and Aboriginal women hold in relation to counselling, the effects of racism and responses to it. We approached people individually, being careful to demonstrate a stance of invitation rather than obligation or demand. All of the women who were approached were enthusiastic and interested in taking part. There was a shared, if tentative, expression by all the women we approached that, in the words of one participant, 'there is some invisibility around race and in [the team I work in] it's not really spoken about'. They felt that the conversations were important to have. In addition to individual interviews with these women, we conducted a definitional ceremony (Myerhoff, 1986; M. White, 2007) involving six participants.

Following the interviews, it was essential to listen to and transcribe people's words accurately. On reviewing the interviews, Alyssha observed that her notes contained her own interpretations and perspectives. Peggy McIntosh (1988), an antiracism activist and author, has written about how white people are raised to see their perspectives as objective and representative of reality. Alyssha realised that this was an assumption that she hadn't confronted in herself. As a result of this observation, we decided to rely on the audio recordings. This also freed Alyssha from taking comprehensive notes and allowed her to focus on the conversations. Participants were emailed the transcripts of their interviews to ensure they accurately reflected our conversations and to allow opportunity to make changes or deletions if desired.

One of the interviews that most stood out to Alyssha included discussion of an event that could easily have been minimised as an experience of racism. This incident highlighted the way that issues of racial domination and power, and therefore the impacts of racism, are present in so many interactions. The worker, Kaya, described a situation in clinical practice where something wasn't handed over to her by another counsellor. Kaya was reprimanded and felt she was being held to account for something that was not her sole responsibility. She reflected through tears that as a woman of colour she would always be positioned as the one in the wrong and considered to be not doing her job well. This was part of a pattern of unfair blaming and subjugation of people of colour.

During this interview, Alyssha sought permission from Kaya to continue despite her tears. Quietly, Kaya said:

> I thought to myself, there's an assumption there that I didn't do it [follow correct procedures], and if it was flipped the other way around, I know I would have been pulled up on it too. I don't know what that assumption was about – if it was because I was new, or that I just didn't follow process or that the white person is [going to be seen as] more competent than I am.

This interview was confronting for both Kaya and Alyssha. Kaya reflected on the difficulty of talking about racism in the workplace, and of discussing the issue with a white person. For Alyssha, discomfort came from knowing that it could have been her asserting privilege and enacting racism. She found herself wanting to minimise Kaya's experience and to defend those involved. She felt raw, but sat with this, reminded by other white people who do this kind of work (DiAngelo, 2011; Land, 2015) that this is the work of white people: to not minimise, but to listen, honour and act. She felt shock, then embarrassment, at her ignorance, shame, deep sadness and defensiveness, even though she knew this exemplified white privilege and power taking space in the room.

Kaya, on reading the interview transcript, reflected that her responses had been vague, and that she had avoided answering questions directly. She explained that these were not issues she or her friends would generally discuss with white people, and to do so had been very challenging. We spoke together about this and issues of safety when talking with white women about issues of race. Kaya was clear she wanted to do the interview again. The following excerpt of our initial conversation captures the tentative nature of Alyssha's enquiries and Kaya's responses.

Kaya: I don't know what that assumption [of sole culpability for the incomplete handover] was about.

Alyssha: If you were to have a gentle guess about what this assumption was about, what might that have you knowing?

Kaya: You'd like to think not...

Alyssha: I've noticed the tentative ways in which these conversations have not wanted to name racism.

Kaya: Yeah, it's not something that I can call out. What am I going to say? What am I going to do about it – because I can't prove it. I think sometimes we feel like we need proof, so I just minimise it.

We ended up having three additional conversations, which worked to structure conversations that were 'safe enough' (Reynolds, 2010). Kaya offered her reflections on this process:

> The group session brought up a whole lot of emotions – more than I was expecting. It was good to be allowed to express these emotions. It's so easy to not talk about racism, to not rock the boat ... To have space to talk with people who get it – who understand the impacts of discrimination, spoken and unspoken – felt really nice.
>
> It was good to see how challenging it felt to talk. Even having the opportunity in the work context was very challenging. Initially I did not feel like addressing it, but I am grateful that I did. It is something that I had not been comfortable talking about before or to a white person – I might have discussions with friends or other people of colour. When talking with white people, I am not sure how much I can say or how openly I can speak. You learn over many, many years not to talk. It can sometimes create tension. So, it's not wanting to have tension, but also not knowing how to talk about it, especially in a workspace where you have a different identity and carry yourself differently. I am not used to being open in that way.

> I think it's great to talk about white privilege – wonderful – as it normalises these topics and creates ease for all involved.
>
> Having a space for self-reflection is good. It was refreshing to hear someone being comfortable in acknowledging her privilege – that things might look fine but that there are people who are in a position of privilege. Really nice to hear that you are not afraid to be outside of your comfort zone. It was really nice modelling for naming white privilege and having healthy discussions about what we have been taught.

Kaya's response prompted further thinking and reflection on our research so far. What had supported Kaya's choice to speak as freely as she did? How could we respond to the vast majority of white people 'who refuse to accept the legitimacy of structural racism and its symptoms' (Eddo-Lodge, 2017, p. ix) to make more of these conversations possible?

Reflections on what enabled these conversations and collaborations with women of colour

Reflecting on the conversations with Kaya, Alyssha went back to listen to and review all of the transcripts. During this process she was also reading Paulo Freire's (2000) work, which talks about solidarity in contexts where one is in the position of oppressor. Freire points out that discovering oneself to be an oppressor may cause considerable anguish, but that this does not necessarily lead to solidarity with people who are oppressed:

> Rationalizing [one's] guilt through paternalistic treatment of the oppressed, all the while holding them fast in a position of dependence, will not do. Solidarity requires that one enter into the situation of those with whom one is solidarity. (Freire, 2000, p. 6)

Here, Alyssha offers some personal reflections on this process of trying to calm her own anguish and enter into a position of solidarity.

She identified the following as having contributed to the interviews going well:

- **Being tentative, curious and aware of the strategic risks people take when speaking** – offering time and space to reflect on what people felt comfortable and interested in talking about.
- **Framing and language** – from the outset, it was made clear that we were inviting people into a conversation about race, racism and white privilege – not a conversation about cultural sensitivity or improving cultural competency, but rather about exploring the unique skills of women of colour in their workplaces. This explicit framing was about contesting the neutrality of these conversations (Coates & Wade, 2004; Reynolds & Richardson/Kianewesquao, 2014).
- **Listening** – it was essential that I listened very actively to hear the women's words and avoid assumptions and judgement. In trying to facilitate multi-storied accounts of women's work, I was reminded of the importance of 'double listening' (M. White, 2003, p. 30) to notice the skills, actions, knowledges or positions that the women were expressing in relation to racism in their lives, and to identify preferred values and commitments (Westmark, Lasse, & Dorte, 2011).
- **Body language** – Kaya reminded me to be aware of my body language. I remember noticing my physical responses and intentionally uncrossing my arms, relaxing my body and really trying to absorb and listen to people's words without judgement or fear.
- **Being comfortable with discomfort** – I made a deep commitment to accepting the perspectives of Aboriginal women and women of colour. This necessitated sitting with uncomfortable feelings and learning about that (polanco, 2013).
- **Connection** – this work was deeply connected to my broader networks of friends, colleagues and activists. These relationships and accountabilities were deeply significant. Their offerings, our

collaborations and our conversations extended my ideas and the work. Narrative practices of valuing partnerships were pivotal (Denborough, 2008; Waldegrave et al., 2003; M. White, 2003).

As we reflected on these interviews, we noticed a number of things we might have done differently. In particular, we would have preferred to enact practices of structuring solidarity (Reynolds & Richardson/ Kianewesquao, 2014) from the beginning of our work together. Following most of the interviews, Alyssha went back and had a brief conversation with the person about her experience of being interviewed. The feedback was that the interviews had the women thinking and put them in places of reflection; that it was good to talk and important to do this work. In future, we would formalise this process of checking in. As a comprehensive way of structuring review, we would use these questions after each interview:

- What has been most interesting about talking about these issues?
- Was there anything you found unhelpful to talk about?
- What is an image or symbol that would describe your experience of this interview?
- If you were to name a hope or value that you connected with during this conversation what would it be?
- Is there a question that would you like to answer that I haven't asked?

What we learnt from the women interviewed

- Speaking about race relations is talking about relations of power.
- Women of colour felt and knew they needed to work twice as hard as their white colleagues.
- The harms that racism does to individuals are tangible to those who experience them and to their communities.

- The burden of dealing with racism should not have to be carried only by women of colour.
- Responses need to go beyond personal acts; collective action is required.
- We need to acknowledge that racism exists in our lives and in the workplace. There need to be structural, organisational and systemic ways to address the issues, as they are systemic and institutional.
- We need to develop ways to speak to the realities of colonisation and the ways that colonisation and colonial ideology is part of this discussion. Everyone in Australia is affected by colonisation.
- Women have diverse and unique cultural skills and practices.
- Women of colour share a sense of connection with clients who aren't white.
- People of colour and Aboriginal clients often express relief and comfort at having a counsellor who is not white. In particular, some Aboriginal women spoke about the importance of not having a white counsellor.
- Unique connections can happen when you are working with someone who might be from your or a similar cultural background.
- Many of the counsellors reflected on how they had expanded their organisations' feminist models by centring the cultural needs of clients.
- Clients connect through sharing cultural understandings, for example asking about family or children as a way of connecting.
- The skills that women of colour hold in counselling are intentionally rendered invisible by whiteness and counselling discourses that don't hold a cultural lens.

- A skill that all the counsellors identified was knowing how to adapt counselling for clients who are not part of the culturally dominant group.
- Knowing how to stand against injustice, in particular when clients speak.
- How invisible skills are undermined by invisible racism that silences and affects how you feel about yourself and your skills – leaving you feeling you have to work harder.
- Skills to identify racism are challenged, not believed. This affects empathy, belief and connection.
- Educating people is a burden.
- Acknowledging Australia's colonial context and the ongoing racism and impacts of colonisation is important to people's current work contexts.
- We should uphold the rights of workers to be safe from racism as a form of violence.

The collective narrative document

Following completion of the interviews and reviewing the transcripts, what stood out was the women's accounts of feeling isolated and separated from other women of colour, and from their broader counselling teams. To address the isolating effects of racism, and to share the women's skills and knowledges through multi-storied accounts of working in sexual assault, we decided to develop a collective narrative document to bring together people's experiences and words (Denborough, 2008).

The collective document we developed was called *Intersectional conversations: Skills, knowledges and practice wisdom of women of colour working in sexual assault*. The document was intended to address two hopes. First, to bring to the fore the work of women of colour and Aboriginal women in responding to sexual assault, making this work more visible for others to learn from. Second, to stand in partnership against the effects of racism and white privilege.

When the document was completed, it was presented to the women involved through a definitional ceremony. Definitional ceremony is a way to respond to 'the problems of invisibility and marginality; they are strategies that provide opportunities for being seen and in one's own terms, garnering witnesses to one's worth, vitality and being' (Myerhoff, 1986, p. 267). As the document was read, the women found strong resonances among the experiences that were included. They had to pause to check whether words were their own or someone else's. There was shared understanding of the struggles, resistance and hopes in their work. Many of the women expressed both relief and grief that others had had similar experiences. The importance of people's cultural knowledge in counselling sessions was affirmed.

At the end of the session, we talked about how the document might be shared and with whom. The women wanted to speak about these issues, but the social cost of talking about racism for a woman of colour is very high and the risks of pointing out discrimination are ever present. It was decided that the collective document would not be shared publicly at this stage, as more work was needed to create safety and collaboration. For now, it would only be shared with the women involved and friends and family of their choosing. The document was especially for them.

Engaging in conversations about white privilege

A number of the women of colour and Aboriginal women whom we had interviewed invited another woman of colour to facilitate a session with them. The aim was to discuss potential next steps without Alyssha's presence. An action arising from this meeting was to prompt us to begin the second part of our research: inviting white women into conversations about responding to racism and addressing privilege.

This work was centrally concerned with honouring and learning from the experiences, skills, knowledge and values of Aboriginal women and other women of colour. However, we were also committed to engaging white women in unpacking whiteness, power and privilege. As we did with our colleagues who were women of colour, we sought to establish partnerships among white women to work towards deconstructing and interrogating the politics of whiteness, in recognition that the denial of power and privilege is one of the most pervasive tools of oppression. In Australia, those of us who are white, culturally dominant people need to acknowledge that our whiteness affords significant privilege; our position of power is assumed and is so much a part of our lives that we rarely think about it. Taliaferro, Casstevens and Gunby (2013) have stated that 'white therapists … cannot intuitively understand the pervasiveness of structural, institutionalised racism and the significance of its impact' (2013, p. 42).

Women of colour should not be further burdened by having to continually raise the subject of racism and educate people about it. In developing this work, we did not want to further burden women of colour and Aboriginal women by positioning them as educators, or by making them responsible for speaking out about racism by sharing individual stories of hardship or racism as a way to educate white people.

During the interviews with women of colour, Alyssha had been privileged and confronted to recognise multiple and diverse ways in which whiteness was ever present in our work, and she needed to bring white women along on this journey. As mentioned above, our ideas on partnership were influenced by the work of the Just Therapy Team, who stipulate that 'no marginalised group should be expected to go into partnership, and no partnership should be entered into without first both groups doing preliminary work to ensure that there is sufficient commitment, common ground and agreement to honour and sustain the partnership' (Waldegrave et al., 2003, p. 115). This preliminary work with white women was much needed.

Alyssha interviewed white sexual assault counsellors and family violence workers using narrative ideas and questions as a guide. She sought to draw out skills and knowledges, to connect to the women's values and hopes for their work and lives, and to build a sense of empowerment to respond to and resist the invisibility of whiteness. Through externalising practices, we hoped we could deconstruct white privilege and invite people to take a position in relation to it (M. White, 2007). The following questions, based on the work of Raheim and colleagues (2004), provided a basis for these interviews:

- Are you interested in having a conversation around privilege and power and particularly white privilege?
- Can you tell me a bit more about what draws your interest to conversations about privilege? And in relation to white privilege particularly?
- Is there a hope or a value in your life more generally that aligns with a commitment to talking about race, racism and privilege?
- How do you think privilege influences your work as a sexual assault counsellor? How do you see that operating? And thinking particularly about white privilege?
- Can you think of a specific time or an example when whiteness or privilege were perhaps present in your work?
- What do you think white privilege has you thinking about yourself or about others?
- What does that say about others?
- Can you share a story from your counselling practice that describes cross-cultural practice that you think went well or that you really learnt something from and that you think might be helpful for other counsellors to know about?
- What skills or knowledge did you draw on to help this to go well?
- Where did those skills, that knowledge, come from? Where did you learn these? From whom?

- What parts of your work practices or intake process do you use or change when working with women of colour? Are there ways that you change your discussions with different clients?
- Do you get asked about your qualifications from clients or colleagues or other professionals?
- Would you like to offer any final comments or reflections?

Prior to issuing invitations to a broader range of white workers, Alyssha decided to interview herself and three white women from her own community. This process was used to refine the interview questions and approach.

Alyssha then conducted four additional interviews with family violence and sexual assault counsellors from across Australia, focusing on the effects of racism, whiteness, privilege and power. An aim was to understand how whiteness is constructed and experienced in work to help dismantle white privilege. Counsellors from sexual assault and family violence settings in Sydney, Bendigo, Footscray and Melbourne were invited to participate. This spread was used to demonstrate that issues of racism and privilege are not unique to any one team or workplace, but are instead a broader social issue. This decision was also intended to support a collective approach for any future actions.

The following is a section from a conversation with one of the participants. It demonstrates the narrative framing of the conversations.

Alyssha: Are you interested in having this conversation around privilege and power and particularly focusing on white privilege?

Georgia: Yes, and it feels like a relief, actually, that we are going to do something within this space, that we are going to do something.

Alyssha: Can you tell me why it is important to you that we are going to do something?

Georgia: Because I think we really need to bring forward this kind of conversation.

Alyssha: Can you tell me a bit more about what draws your interest to conversations on privilege particularly?

Georgia: Well, I think for me, being a white, middle-class woman working in an organisation, I have some privilege.

Alyssha: Thinking about this privilege, I am interested to hear why you wanted to talk about white privilege?

Georgia: What draws me to have a conversation is to be open and honest and look at the way that [white privilege] impacts everybody. Having a conversation and not making any assumptions of what that's like. If we are to going be able to work in an accountable and inclusive way, we really have to have these conversations and to do our thinking. We talk a lot about trauma theory, and there are shared understandings and conversations around the impacts of trauma, but it's not often in this organisation that we talk about the impact of race. But that's what is actually being presented to us all the time … it impacts on someone's total experiences of violence and trauma. I see it as just as important as any other aspect of trauma, but it doesn't get nearly as much airtime, and I don't think I have established my thinking around that in the same ways. There is an uncomfortableness in that for me.

Alyssha: This uncomfortableness, can you tell me some more about its role in this for you?

Georgia: It would involve acknowledging how bad we are talking about it, or what we are not doing. So, there is a kind of shame around that. It's almost like we have gone past it and decided that we don't need to talk about it anymore.

Ongoing work

> I am not free while any woman is unfree, even when her shackles are very different from my own. And I am not free as long as one person of color remains chained. Nor is any one of you. (Audre Lorde, 1981, p. 131)

This work is a long-term process of collaboration and partnership. In this chapter we have described ways that individual and collective narrative practices, informed by the work of decolonising theorists, can be used to engage with racism and work towards dismantling white privilege. The work described was generated from many conversations between people working in the violence prevention and response sectors. We are grateful for their willingness to be involved, and for their honest explorations of their work and how it intersects with racism and white privilege.

Our goal was to bring forward experiences, hopes, skills and knowledges of women of colour and Aboriginal women by witnessing and documenting their stories of practice and resistance. We also sought to engage white women in deconstructing and dismantling white privilege. The work of this project has involved constant reflection, change and action. As Jalendar, one of the women involved in the project, stated, 'the next steps will be to create some kind of movement from here with [our] wider team(s)'. Our efforts to interrogate white privilege will continue through a commitment to longer-term processes of challenge and collaboration with the teams in our workplaces and sector to address racism and respond to privilege in meaningful, sustaining and sustainable ways. This ongoing project would not be possible without the partnerships that have been built and sustained. An ethic of togetherness was a key reason that we wanted to do this work. It was an attempt to stand in solidarity with all Aboriginal peoples and people of colour. We drew on the work of Vicki Reynolds (2012), who has written that solidarity:

speaks to an understanding that just ways of being are interconnected, as are our struggles and sites of resistance. We are meant to do this work together. The work of justice-doing is profoundly collaborative and there are many paths. (Reynolds, 2012, p. 5)

Suggestions for others who wish to introduce difficult conversations about racism and white privilege in their workplace or sector

Here are some ideas that we consider useful for engaging in this sort of project.

- Employing narrative practices of double listening, re-authoring and creating space to examine the effects of the problem was useful for these conversations.
- Take the work slowly and carefully, structure safety and build relationships, connections, friendship and partnerships.
- White people considering this work must do so in partnership with people of colour or Aboriginal people.
- Incorporate conversations about white privilege and power. These are crucial but often forgotten in work to address and respond to racism.
- There must be acknowledgment that in the workplace, race-based discrimination can occur at individual, interpersonal and systemic levels. Racism is frequently experienced in workplaces (Trenerry, Franklin, & Paradies, 2012).
- As a response to the above, organisational commitment and resourcing is needed. For example, time dedicated to the project and space in meetings to talk about responding to racism and addressing privilege.
- It is important for white people to practice sitting with any sadness, fear or anger. Do not minimise people's experiences, be defensive or try to explain racism away. There is no space to deny or contest the realities and impacts of racism.

- Find ways to ensure that less work and responsibility is placed on people of colour to raise issues of race and racism.
- Ensure that responsibility is taken by white people to collaborate with other white people to address racism.

Looking back, looking forward

As we look back and look forward, it seems appropriate to close with Simangaliso's words.

> Before working on this project, I was carrying so many untold stories from my grandparents, my parents and also my own stories. It is the burden of these experiences that has been the driver of this work. The experiences have been passed on from generation to generation. I was raised by a proud, strong family who had been colonised to believe that white people are better, and I embodied that, explicitly and implicitly. I have worked so hard to fit in, to be closer to whiteness and shun my own heritage. This is the history, present tense and ongoing legacy of colonisation. I was raised to never question what a white person says nor to challenge them. The message was that you have to make it your duty to please a white person, to behave in a way that meets their standards. I am therefore on a journey of decolonising my mind.
>
> When this project first started, I don't think I fully comprehended what was about to unfold personally, politically and spiritually. When I started working as a counsellor in family violence and sexual assault, I was the only woman of colour. I struggled with many things but had no words to express what I was struggling with. This project has provided me space and safety to voice what I have carried for so many years in isolation. I feel more empowered now than ever. I speak up now more often than not about racism and white privilege in settings where I am usually the minority, with my voice shaking at times because

I don't want to be known as the 'shit stirrer' and I don't want to make anyone uncomfortable. My speaking up has come at a price but the price I pay for being quiet is greater still.
Racism exists. I have experienced it in many workplaces from clients, from colleagues and from managers. Some of it was overt, some subtle, but every experience shaped me. Without first calling out white privilege, we can't call out racism. I was working in a place where it was assumed that I was treated equally to my white colleagues which was not the case. We might have worked the same hours at the same place for the same pay but we were not equal in so many ways. The number of times I get asked where my accent is from, how long I have been in Australia, what my qualifications are, means that I work longer hours, and work harder. The emotional and spiritual toil is immeasurable. So, no, we are not equal in that sense. I strongly feel that it is every individual and counsellor's responsibility to come together in solidarity to acknowledge this lack of equality and to work together to dismantle racism and white privilege.

I have lost count of the number of times I have had my experiences of racism minimised or dismissed. Incidents are so hard to call out. I have suffered things in isolation, and I didn't realise the magnitude of the accumulated harm of racism and white privilege. This is only the beginning of this work and I would love to form more partnerships and to work with as many people as possible on these conversations about ending discrimination, oppression and injustice.

References

Australian Human Rights Commission. (2019). *Racism stops with me.* Retrieved from https://itstopswithme.humanrights.gov.au/about-racism

Blair, K., Dunn, K., Kamp, A., & Alam, O. (2017). *Challenging Racism Project 2015–16 national survey report.* Sydney, Australia: Western Sydney University

Chilisa, B. (2012). *Indigenous research methodologies.* London, England: Sage.

Coates, L., & Wade, A. (2004). Telling it like it isn't: Obscuring perpetrator responsibility for violent crime. *Discourse and Society, 15*(5), 499–526.

Crenshaw, K. (1989). Demarginalizing the intersection of race and sex: A Black feminist critique of antidiscrimination doctrine, feminist theory and antiracist politics. *University of Chicago Legal Forum,* (1), 139–168.

Denborough, D. (2008). *Collective narrative practice: Responding to individuals, groups and communities who have experienced trauma.* Adelaide, Australia: Dulwich Centre Publications.

Denborough, D. (2012). A storyline of collective narrative practice: A history of ideas, social projects and partnerships. *International Journal of Narrative Therapy and Community Work,* (1), 40–65.

DiAngelo, R. (2011). White fragility. *International Journal of Critical Pedagogy, 3*(3), 54–70.

Eddo-Lodge, R. (2017). *Why I'm no longer talking to white people about race.* London, England: Bloomsbury.

Frankenberg, R. (1993). *The social construction of Whiteness: White women, race matters.* Minneapolis: University of Minnesota Press.

Freedman, J. (2011). My favourite questions. *International Journal of Narrative Therapy and Community Work,* (4), 3–8.

Freire, P. (2000). *Pedagogy of the oppressed.* New York, NY: Continuum.

Hewitt, L., & Worth, C. (2014). *Victims like us: The development of the Victorian CASAs.* Retrieved from https://www.casa.org.au/about-us/victims-like-us-the-development-of-the-victorian-casas/

Land, C. (2015). *Decolonizing solidarity.* London, England: Zed.

Lorde, A. (1981). *Sister outsider: Essays and speeches.* Berkeley, CA: Crossing.

McIntosh, P. (1988). *White privilege: Unpacking the invisible knapsack.* Retrieved from https://www.winnipeg.ca/clerks/boards/citizenequity/pdfs/white_privilege.pdf

Moreton-Robinson, A. (2000). *Talkin up to the white woman.* Brisbane, Australia: Queensland University Press.

Morgan, A. (2000). *What is narrative therapy? An easy to read introduction.* Adelaide, Australia: Dulwich Centre Publications.

Myerhoff, B. (1982). Life history among the elderly: Performance, visibility, and re-membering. In J. Ruby (Ed.), *A crack in the mirror: Reflective perspectives in anthropology* (pp. 99–117). Philadelphia: University of Pennsylvania Press.

Myerhoff, B. (1986). 'Life not death in Venice': Its second life. In V. Turner & E. Bruner (Eds.), *The anthropology of experience* (pp. 261–286). Chicago, IL: University of Illinois Press.

Our Watch. (2018). *Our Watch.* Retrieved from: https://www.ourwatch.org.au/Understanding-Violence/Facts-and-figures

polanco, m. (2013, January 24). *Colouring narrative therapy's solidarity by marcela polanco* [Video file]. Retrieved from https://dulwichcentre.com.au/colouring-narrative-therapys-solidarity-by-marcela-polanco/

Raheim, S., White, C., Denborough, D., Waldegrave, C., Tamasese, K., Tuhaka, F., Frankin, A., Fox, H., & Carey, M. (2004). *An invitation to narrative practitioners to address privilege and dominance.* Retrieved from https://dulwichcentre.com.au/a-continuing-invitation-to-narrative-practitioners-to-address-privilege-and-dominance/

Reynolds, V. (2010). Doing justice: A witnessing stance in therapeutic work alongside survivors of torture and political violence. In J. Raskin, S. Bridges, & R. Neimeyer (Eds.), *Studies in meaning 4: Constructivist perspectives on theory, practice, and social justice* (pp. 157–184) New York, NY: Pace University Press.

Reynolds, V. (2012). An ethical stance for justice-doing in community work and therapy. *Journal of Systemic Therapies*, *31*(4), 18–33.

Reynolds, V., & Richardson/Kianewesquao, C. (2014). Structuring safety in therapeutic work alongside Indigenous survivors of residential schools. *Canadian Journal of Native Studies*, *34*(2), 147.

Ridgeway, A. (2015, April). *Improving cross cultural practice: Strategies and resources for working with women from CALD backgrounds* [Video file]. Retrieved from https://www.1800respect.org.au/all-past-webinars/improving-cross-cultural-practice-april-2015/

Ridler, C. (2018). *Queer and trans Indigenous and/or people of colour (QTIPoC) Project*. Retrieved from http://www.switchboard.org.au/qtipoc-project/

Russell, S., & Carey, M. (2004). *Narrative therapy: Responding to your questions.* Adelaide, Australia: Dulwich Centre Publications.

Sherwood, J., & Edwards, T. (2006). Decolonisation: A critical step for improving Aboriginal health. *Contemporary Nurse*, *22*(2), 178–190. doi: 10.5172/conu.2006.22.2.178

Taliaferro, J., Casstevens, W., & Gunby, D. (2013). Working with African American clients using narrative therapy: An operational citizenship and critical race theory framework. *International Journal of Narrative Therapy and Community Work*, (1), 34–45.

Trenerry, B., Franklin, H., & Paradies, Y. (2012). *Preventing race-based discrimination and supporting cultural diversity in the workplace: An evidence review: Full report.* Melbourne Australia: Victorian Health Promotion Foundation. Retrieved from https://www.vichealth.vic.gov.au/~/media/resourcecentre/publicationsandresources/economic%20participation/2012%20workplace/chw_discrim_full_web_final.ashx

Tuhiwai Smith, L. (2012). *Decolonizing methodologies: Research and Indigenous peoples.* London, England: Zed.

Vic Health. (2019). *Australian's attitudes to violence against women.* Retrieved from https://www.vichealth.vic.gov.au/media-and-resources/publications/2013-national-community-attitudes-towards-violence-against-women-survey

Vic Health Koori Research and Community Development. (2000). *We don't like research… But in Koori hands it could make a difference.* Melbourne, Australia: Author. Retrieved from http://onemda.unimelb.edu.au/sites/default/files/docs/CR1-WeDontLike%20Research.pdf

Waldegrave, C., Tamasese, K., Tuhaka, F., & Campbell, W. (2003). *Just Therapy – A journey.* Adelaide, Australia: Dulwich Centre Publications.

Westmark, T., Lasse, O., & Dorte, N. (2011). The complexity of listening – listening for complexity: Narrative consultancy work in organisations. *Explorations,* (1), 21–35.

White, C. (2016). *A memory book for the field of narrative practice.* Adelaide, Australia: Dulwich Centre Publications.

White, M. (2003). Narrative practice and community assignments. *International Journal of Narrative Therapy and Community Work,* (2), 17–55.

White, M. (2007). *Maps of narrative practice.* New York, NY: Norton.

White, M., & Epston, D. (1990). *Narrative means to therapeutic ends.* New York, NY: Norton.

Wingard, B., & Lester, J. (2001). *Telling our stories in ways that make us stronger.* Adelaide, Australia: Dulwich Centre Publications.

Narrative approaches to restorative justice settings:

Considerations of power, struggle and social transformation

Renee Handsaker

Introduction

The restorative justice work I am involved in brings together a person who has caused death or serious injury through dangerous driving and the 'victim(s)', including bereaved loved ones. Restorative justice has a wide range of applications, and in this context it seeks to provide an opportunity for the person who has been impacted to give voice to their experience of the harm done, and to discuss with the person responsible what future steps might be taken to respond to that harm. This work demands rigour, accountability and the ongoing interrogation and articulation of the guiding vision and principles of restorative processes. I view this work through a feminist lens focused on considerations of power, struggle and social transformation. This has led to questioning reliance on police and prisons to resolve harm and conflict, and raises concerns about how these structures perpetrate discrimination and oppression, and often inflame conflict.

In this chapter, I explore the process of facilitating restorative justice conferences using tools from narrative practice. My hope in writing about this work is to encourage others – particularly those who wish to respond to harm without relying on discourses of shame and punishment – to consider the adaptation of such practices and principles to their own contexts. These ideas are explored through the stories of two restorative conferences that I facilitated. Although they shared similar themes, each was shaped by its specific context and considerations. This chapter sets out the narrative principles that informed my work in the lead-up to and during these two conferences, and reflects on some of the complexities that emerged. In addition, my use of narrative practices is demonstrated through the inclusion of transcripts and details of questions posed during the process.

Restorative processes: exploring alternatives to adversarial justice systems

Restorative justice is a term applied to a diverse array of processes. They share a common framework for thinking about how to respond to acts of harm or 'wrongdoing'. Restorative justice is interested in relationships among humans and the impact of harm on individuals and communities (Zehr, 2002).

Restorative justice processes are often guided by the following questions:

- Who has been harmed?
- What are their needs?
- Whose obligations are these?
- What is an appropriate process, involving stakeholders, to respond to these needs and obligations? (Zehr, 2002)

Restorative justice frameworks have grown out of recognition of the limitations and failures of the Western legal system that so often deepens societal wounds rather than contributing to peace and healing. It could be argued that there is very little about our current criminal justice system that contributes to conflict resolution, healing and peace. In his book *Beyond the prison*, David Denborough (1996) argued that 'we live in a punitive culture – one that equates justice with revenge, in which many relationships end in retribution, and in which ways of addressing conflict often inflame anguish rather than diminish it' (Denborough, 1996, p. 98). This all too often results in people who have experienced harm feeling neglected, ignored or even further harmed by the adversarial nature of the criminal justice process, which encourages denial, conflict and defensiveness. Unquestioned reliance on the criminal justice system to settle our conflicts means that many of us remain entirely invested in the idea that this system delivers justice, even when people are deeply harmed by the experience. A further taken-for-granted idea that permeates our society is that those responsible for enacting wrongdoing or harm must be punished. Denborough (1996) argued that:

> perhaps the more serious the offence, the more an alternative, community-building and restorative approach is required. It may also be true that, at times of profound grief, outrage and anger, perhaps the least healing response is that which is offered by the police, courts and prison – confrontation and retribution. (Denborough, 1996, p. 219)

We must ask ourselves what effects this discourse of punishment and retribution has on our capacity to heal, recover and transform relationships characterised by acts of harm. Can we imagine processes that would build relationships after an act of harm, rather than forcing those involved even further apart?

It is also significant to recognise that the criminal justice system disproportionately punishes particular groups in our community. Sarah Schulman (2016), in *Conflict is not abuse,* argued that police and prisons have repeatedly been shown to be structurally opposed to queer, black and feminist people and interests. These communities have extensive insider knowledge about responding to such systems, and rich histories of creating processes for addressing harm within their communities without reliance on the state-based responses of police or prisons.

The development of alternative mechanisms for addressing harm by these communities has led to the movement for transformative justice (Dixon & Piepzna-Samarasinha, 2020). In my work facilitating restorative processes, I draw on a number of transformative justice principles. Transformative justice extends a restorative justice approach by seeking to transform unjust relations of power. It seeks not only to address the conflict between a person who has harmed and a person who has been harmed, but also the social and structural context that has influenced the harm (Kim, 2018). To assist with this, I have drawn on the work of a number of community organisations that have developed approaches to accountability, interrupting harm and transformative processes, such as those documented by Creative Interventions (2018)[1] in their StoryTelling and Organizing Project. The ideas documented by Generation Five[2] (2018) in their *Transformative Justice Handbook* have also been very useful. Generation Five debunk the idea that punishment is a necessary ingredient for changing the behaviour of someone who has caused harm, arguing that:

> most of us have been deeply shaped by the false notion that in order for people to behave better, they need to feel worse. In practice we see that humans are more likely to change in desirable ways when they are more resourced, not less. (Generation Five, 2018, p. 53)

In developing my own understanding of these concepts, I have particularly appreciated the idea that:

> by standing for everyone's need for healing, we challenge the dehumanising logic that is central to systems of oppression, domination and abuse. By standing for everyone's need for healing, we maintain our commitment to a vision of true liberation. (Generation Five, 2018, p. 56)

This commitment to 'standing for everyone's healing' is something I sought to bring into my work with Simon and Josie.

Restorative process 1: Simon and Josie

Simon was driving back from a pub in regional Australia. He had drunk more than the legal limit of alcohol and was found to have been travelling at almost double the speed limit. He lost control of the car, veered on to the wrong side of the road and collided with an oncoming car. The oncoming car was driven by Gordon Walker. Gordon died in the collision. Simon was sentenced to six years and four months in prison, with a non-parole period of four years. Gordon's sister, Josie, contacted a local organisation that she knew worked with restorative justice principles and requested a conference with Simon. Josie wanted to meet with Simon for a couple of reasons. The first was that this was something her brother would have wanted her to do. Secondly, she wanted to make sure Simon understood the gravity of the situation and that he would commit to changing his ways in the future. The organisation made contact with Simon who agreed to participate in a meeting with Josie. This was when my involvement began.

Power relations and considerations of context

In approaching this work, it was important to consider the power relations and ethical questions raised by the context Simon and Josie had found themselves in. A narrative approach sees problems, and therefore problems of harm, as existing within cultural contexts. These contexts include power relations relating to race, class, sexuality, gender and disadvantage (Morgan, 2000). It was thus important that I considered how relationships of power might operate between Simon and Josie. There are always multiple operations of power in any relationship. A significant power relation in this context was that Simon had already been subjected to a criminal trial process and was incarcerated. The court had handed down its version of accountability and punishment and it was important to ensure that the conference process did not serve as a reinscription of the legal proceedings. I needed to be careful to ensure that this process would not be a new way to punish Simon under a different guise. It was crucial that, as Simon was incarcerated at the time and given the nature of prisons and the relationships of oppression and power that are fundamental to their operation, I proceeded carefully to ensure Simon could freely agree or decline to participate in this process and would in no way be coerced.

I also needed to think about Simon's physical and emotional safety, and to avoid having him participate in an emotionally taxing experience only to return to a cell on his own. The words of Blanche, in an interview with Denborough (1996), highlight the risk therapists can pose to people who are incarcerated, while putatively helping them:

> You can't dig deep into somebody's psyche and then send them back to the wing after an hour … you start unravelling bits of what has happened to them ... and you're left to brood on that … while the prison whittles away your other defences. (Blanche, quoted in Denborough, 1996, p. 93)

Denborough (1996) continued:

> prison is a place in which those incarcerated have to shut down and protect themselves, both from others and from overwhelming feelings of worthlessness, in order to survive. It is hardly an environment that facilitates prisoners being able to open themselves up to the feelings of others. As professionals we leave the prison each night, and those with whom we are working return to cells and a system designed to punish and prey upon feelings of guilt and worthlessness. (Denborough, 1996, p. 94)

In this work it is important to be alert to how professionals, such as myself, can so easily become coopted and unintentionally collude with imprisoning practices that result in the dispossession of spirit, self-worth and hope for the future. In this instance, I needed to ensure that any process Simon participated in was ultimately invigorating and sustaining of his own values, identity and hopes, and to avoid further depleting his connections to them.

An additional contextual factor, one of pivotal importance, was that Simon's actions had resulted in someone's life being lost. It was important to ask myself how this loss of life could be honoured for Josie, who had lost a loved one so unexpectedly and in this way. How could we ensure that the legacy of Gordon was honoured during and by this process? I find hope in the work of Frank Ostaseski (2017) who described the transformative power of death as he reflected on his years of working with individuals and families during and after death. He has suggested that we can 'harness the awareness of death to appreciate the fact that we are alive, to encourage self exploration, to clarify our values, to find meaning, and to generate positive action' (2017, p. 3). Ostaseski's ideas have encouraged me to consider that where there has been death, openings may still be created for those experiencing the loss. Perhaps there are special possibilities for transforming a context of harm through a restorative process where there has been the loss of a loved one. It may be possible to look beyond the impositions created by discourses of punishment towards connection with what is most cherished and precious, and that this reconnection may ultimately be a more helpful way forward for the person experiencing loss, and more honouring of the person whose life was lost.

With these guiding intentions and hopes in mind, I set about preparing to bring Simon and Josie together. Over the course of several months, there were a number of phone calls, followed by one face-to-face meeting with each of them to prepare for coming together.

Transforming the experience and effects of harm

The unexpected loss of a loved one can have profound and devastating effects. It can permeate every tentacle of life and very often leaves someone in a debilitating state of shock, sadness and anger. Although the person who has enacted harm needs to be responsible and accountable for the harm that has occurred, there can also be debilitating and destructive consequences for that person's life, particularly in the context of dangerous driving, when it is most often the case that the person had not intended to take the life of another. Crippling guilt and identity conclusions of worthlessness are common in this context. The stories we tell ourselves about the harm we've enacted or experienced influence our identities and therefore our capacity for learning, healing and wellbeing. What I describe as 'transforming the experience and effects of harm' is an effort to address and respond to a person's current understanding of, and ongoing relationship to, the harm that has taken place. This includes the person's understandings of and relationship to the person or people who were harmed: a relationship that is singularly characterised and defined by the incident of harm.

A powerful way we can do this is to create opportunities to re-author, expand and change the stories we tell ourselves, including the stories we tell ourselves about the other person. Each person who has been affected by the harm can be offered opportunities to develop new meanings and expanded storylines. These new understandings, developed through expanded storylines, may provide a preferred position in which to stand in relation to the harm that has been done. This repositioning in relation to the harm can happen when each participant is given the opportunity to tell stories in personally resonant ways, while the facilitator elevates points of resonance between participants' own stories and the storylines of the other (Denborough, 2011). The current experience and effects of harm can be transformed by the storylines that become available to understand it.

Once again, Creative Interventions (2018) informed my thinking as I sought to transform the experience and effects of harm. By following their principles of directly linking expanding options and opportunities for safety with the capacity to take risks, new opportunities for transformation were created.

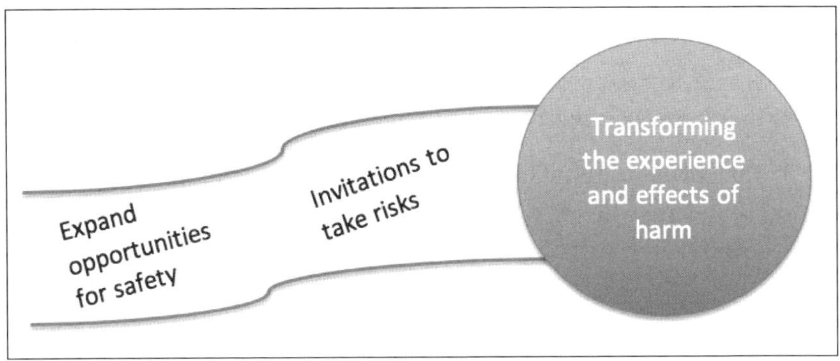

Figure 1. Transforming the experience and effects of harm in restorative processes

Expanding options and opportunities for safety

I particularly appreciate how the idea that expanding options and opportunities for safety doesn't imply that safety is a fixed state of being. Rather, it is recognised as requiring constant renegotiation through questions and conversations. Addressing the topic of safety, Generation Five's *Transformative justice handbook* states that:

> safety is not a 'state' to arrive at, but a dynamic set of questions, choices and skills that allow each of us to exercise agency: making choices, owning those choices, reflecting upon the outcomes of those choices, and letting our learning inform future actions. (Generation Five, 2018, p. 39)

In my preparatory meetings with Simon and Josie, I sought to expand options and opportunities for safety through enquiring about their needs, preferences, skills, hopes and fears. I invited Josie to imagine sitting across from Simon and asked about worries or concerns that she might have. When she told me she was concerned that he would sit silently and not say anything, I asked a series of questions designed to bring forward options available to her, and to demonstrate that her choices could guide our next steps:

- If that were to happen, would you still want to go ahead with the meeting?
- If that happens, what would you like me to do?
- If that happens, how can you stay connected with or hold on to a sense of who you are, what you care about and what you know about yourself?

Invitation to take risks

Jeanette Winterson has also written on the relationship between safety and taking risks. She reasoned that safety does not come without risk, and that risk itself illuminates what we value (Winterson, 2001). Winterson's sentiment uncovers possibilities for exploring 'absent but implicit' (White, 2000) values, hopes and commitments that underpin participants' decisions to take part in the process. Through rendering visible the risks Simon and Josie were taking, and what was absent yet implicit in their decisions to take part, new opportunities for re-authoring single-storied versions of themselves were made possible. These stories illuminated what Simon and Josie each gave value to. Their accounts of committing to proceed with this meeting, despite the risks of further distress, invited the sharing of additional stories about the people in their lives who might join with them in these values and hopes.

Throughout this process I extended the invitation to take risks to myself. Bringing people together under such difficult and splintering circumstances can definitely feel risky. At times I felt the weight of not wanting to 'mess it up', and was concerned that I might do further harm during the process. This was countered by the idea that there might also be risk in leaving people with distressing and unhelpful single-storied versions of themselves, the other person and the incident of harm. It is, of course, important to acknowledge that there was also risk in *not* providing the opportunity for Simon and Josie to have a conversation with each other, a consideration that could all too easily be overlooked, (D. Denborough, personal communication, August, 2018). I found particular inspiration in Sharon Welch's (1990) 'feminist ethic of risk', which spurred me on in moments of worry and doubt. Welch has argued that 'responsible action does not mean the certain achievement of desired ends but the creation of a matrix in which further actions are possible, the creation of the conditions of possibility for desired changes' (1990, p. 20). At times when the responsibility of doing no further harm has felt overwhelming, I have been comforted by the idea that this work prioritises movement towards preferred goals and by Welch's position that we can choose 'to care and to act although there are no guarantees of success' (1990, p. 68).

Preparatory conversations

During our conversations in the lead-up to the conference, I drew on understandings from narrative practice. I understand these practices to be linked to the expansion of safety. The following are neither verbatim transcripts nor an exhaustive list of narrative practices and questions used. My aim is to provide readers with a snapshot of what happened during a series of conversations that took place over a three-month period.

Testing out opportunities for alternative meanings

In order to identify opportunities for the generation of alternative meanings, I adopted a 'willingness to listen for cracks or openings in the conflict story' (Winslade, 2009, p. 567). In my meeting with Simon, I learnt that he was convinced that Josie and her family members would detest him, be angry and want to yell, and that they would be happy to see him locked away in prison. This was a painful conclusion for Simon to consider living out for the rest of his life. For Josie, it was the absence of a story of Simon that felt difficult. She had no knowledge of what he looked like, no sense of who he was or what he was like. The only information she had was from the court sentencing transcripts. Simon remained an invisible yet powerful entity that caused her pain because she had no way to integrate a storyline of Simon with what had happened. Through these preparatory conversations I began to see significant potential for re-storying the meanings that had developed for both Simon and Josie.

Inviting re-tellings of what the person holds dear

A key hope for inviting re-tellings of what Simon and Josie held dear was to identify fertile ground for re-authoring conversations (White, 2007) that could be revisited and built on throughout this process. An additional hope was to build a foundation for Simon and Josie to stand on prior to traversing more painful and difficult areas of discussion. Sue Mitchell (2006) has discussed how people who have experienced traumatic events can be 'invited to re-tell their story from the perspective of a safer ground, a different territory of identity than that evoked by the traumatic experience' (2006, p. 105). This is what I sought to achieve for Simon and Josie.

I invited Simon and Josie to share with me the values, beliefs and hopes that underpinned their participation in this process.

Renee: Simon, you had a belief going into this process that Josie would want to yell and abuse you – and despite this you agreed to participate. Why is it important to you to participate in this conference? And was the decision to participate an easy or a difficult one?

When Simon replied that it had been an easy decision to make because he believed it was the right thing to do, I invited him to thicken this story by enquiring about the history of this value. I asked him who else would know that 'doing the right thing' was important to him. Were there other people in his family who came to mind when he spoke of knowing something was the right thing to do?

Renee: Josie, imagine yourself six months after the conference. You look back at the conference and are able to feel a real sense of pride in your participation. What is it you have conveyed to Simon, and what values would you be expressing in doing this?

I went on to ask Josie about the history of the values she spoke of, and whether they were values she shared with her brother, Gordon. We also spent time reflecting on who Gordon was, what values and beliefs were important to him and if there were ways she might be able to honour Gordon's values and beliefs in this process.

Making both participants' skills and knowledges accessible to them

In difficult times, it is easy to become separated from the skills, knowledges and learnings that we have previously accessed and relied on in our lives. Through reconnecting Simon and Josie to their own skills and knowledges, my hope was to return this 'conflict' to the original owners of it, so Simon and Josie could decide on the most meaningful and personally resonant ways for them to progress. Simon spoke of his fear of 'shutting down' in the conference, or of getting his words jumbled, and that Josie would interpret this as him not caring. One of his biggest worries throughout our preparatory conversations was that he would not be able to articulate himself clearly and that this would confirm Josie's belief that he was 'a piece of shit' who didn't care about what he had done. We spent a good deal of time talking about how he might recognise when 'shutting down' was happening, and whether there were ways I could help him be on the lookout for 'shutting down'. In doing so, I enquired about what Simon knew about 'shutting down', when it happened and what past experience had taught him he might need in order to help him find his words again.

Sharing information between Simon and Josie

Gaining permission to share some of what I learnt in my conversations with the other participant was important to preparing both parties for the meeting. I was deliberate and influential in choosing the information I shared with each participant. I was particularly interested in discovering and highlighting shared ground or hopes, in particular vulnerabilities and anxieties that might elicit compassion and understanding from the other, and in territory where seeds of alternative narratives and meanings might be planted. An additional purpose in sharing information between participants was to aid any possibility for the 'conflict narrative' to lose momentum prior to participants coming together (Winslade, 2009). With Simon's permission, I shared with Josie his worry about 'shutting down' and not being able to articulate himself, and his concern that Josie would interpret this as him not caring. I relayed what I had learnt from my conversations with Simon: that it was important to him to show her that he did care. Together, Josie and I spent time thinking about how she might react if Simon did 'shut down' and she wasn't able to get the answers she desired. I also shared with Josie that Simon had developed a strategy of 'taking some time out' to collect himself and I obtained Josie's agreement that she would be understanding if Simon needed this option on the day. Josie said it was helpful to know this prior to going in to the conference as it would help her understand and interpret Simon's actions more accurately.

Listening for shared territories and possible places of joining

In my conversations with Simon and Josie, both expressed a desire to help the other. They also shared a hope for change in Simon's life. When I hear of shared hopes it alerts me to possibilities for contribution. Denborough (2008) has written of the helpful effects of 'enabling contribution' and facilitating opportunities for individuals and communities who are going through hard times to make contributions to others who are going through similar difficulties. I wondered whether Simon and Josie would be able to contribute to one another's lives, or the lives of others.

Doing no further harm and taking care

Dominant social and cultural narratives about what constitutes justice have a significant influence on the way those who have enacted harm think about what they 'deserve' and how they expect to be treated. Simon believed that Josie would be very angry at him and it was okay with him if she wanted to yell and scream at him. I was able to convey to Simon about Josie's wish to have a respectful conversation, and that her hope for the meeting was to be able to ask some questions. I also reiterated to Simon that behaviour experienced by either party as threatening or intimidating would not be allowed in this process. Simon seemed surprised, but somewhat relieved, by this information.

A further demonstration of the careful preparation involved was the negotiation of who should begin the conversation, what questions would be asked and what areas of conversation were comfortable enough for both participants to navigate. It is important in my work that the preparation serves to minimise surprises and alleviate the almost inevitable anxieties or concerns that arise when two people meet for the first time under such difficult circumstances.

Inviting others to join the conversation

With permission from Simon and Josie, a further important aspect of this process was to extend an invitation to others who may have been impacted to join the process. Simon decided there was no-one from his family, friendship or broader community who he would like to invite; he preferred that Jenna, his custodial officer, be invited to attend the conference as a support person for him. Simon had a trusting relationship with Jenna that felt comfortable to him. We invited Jenna into the process, and she joined us for the face-to-face preparation meeting. I was a little tentative about how the inherent imbalance of power in their relationship might operate, and with what effects, but I was also pleased to hear that Simon had established trust with someone inside the prison who would be able to support him. Josie was also clear there was no-one else she wanted in the room for her meeting with Simon, but we did organise that her partner would travel with her and offer support once the conference was over.

Restorative conference: Simon and Josie come together

One of the challenges in undertaking the conference inside prison walls was a lack of influence over the physical space. Prison staff determined that a family visiting room would be used. The room was far from ideal. It was small and furnished with two frayed leather couches, plastic chairs, a sink and a double bed. I wondered how this rather odd setting might affect Josie and Simon's sense of comfort as they navigated what was going to be an uncomfortable conversation.

In the preparatory conversations I had introduced narrative practices that support the expansion of safety, risk taking and possibilities for transforming harm. The diagram below illustrates how incorporating additional narrative practices into restorative processes can powerfully contribute to the transformation of harm. I attempted to bring these narrative themes into focus during the conference and used them as a guiding map for traversing difficult territories.

Locating harm in the social context

To locate the harm in the social context, I invited Simon to begin the conference by describing himself a little – his family and what life was like leading up to the collision. Simon described a lot of family pressure leading up to the accident and spoke of drinking very heavily on a day-to-day basis. He talked about working in scaffolding and how he had been

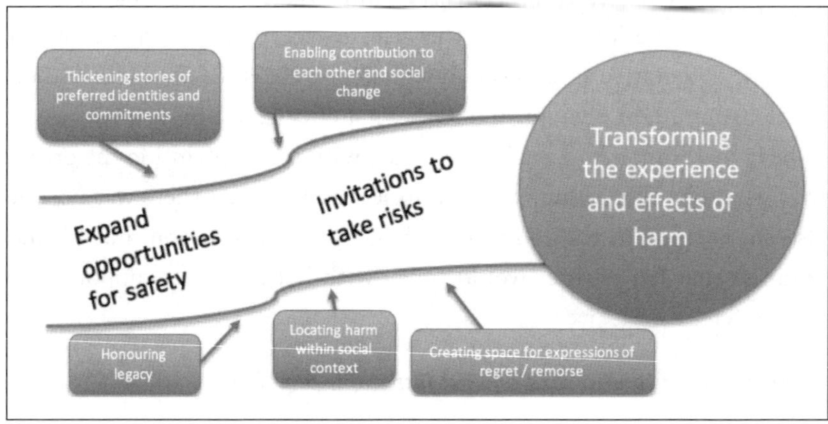

Figure 2. Incorporating narrative themes to transform the experience and effects of harm in restorative processes

instructed that in construction work there was an expectation to drink every day – and this was a message he took seriously. He reflected that it wasn't uncommon for him to drink a slab a day. He explained how his father had never told him not to drink and drive: drinking and driving was something that his father did and his father didn't want to be a hypocrite. It is pertinent to note here that striving to render visible social and structural contexts presents a tension in this work. Because people from backgrounds that carry certain disadvantages are overrepresented in the criminal justice system, it is a particular ethic of this work to find ways to bring broader structural and systemic effects and considerations into the conversation. However, it has been my experience that people who have been impacted by harm are sometimes sensitive to what they perceive to be 'excuses'. An ongoing dilemma is how to locate harm in a social and structural context without diminishing responsibility and accountability.

Thickening stories of preferred identities and commitments

During the conference, Josie raised the concern that when Simon was released he would be going back to the same situation and experience the same 'triggers', which might cause him to start drinking again. When Josie asked Simon how he planned to resist these triggers, he spoke of his commitment to not going back to his 'old ways' and of the people he had on the outside who would be able to help him resist taking up drinking again. Josie appeared frustrated by the lack of detail Simon was providing about his plans to resist his old ways and relayed that if he went back into exactly the same environment she found it difficult to believe that anything would be different. Simon replied that his family was his family, and he couldn't just go and get himself a new one.

At this point, I found it necessary to become more influential in the conversation to help strengthen the narrative of Simon's commitment to not going back to old ways. I asked Simon who in his family and community circle might join with him in this commitment to resisting his old ways: Who would be excited to hear him talk in this way? Who might he call on for support if he found himself in danger of slipping into old ways? Simon named some of his friends, his mum and his cousin as people he could turn to for support and who would 'get behind' his new commitments. I asked Simon to consider whether there were other things he might need on the outside to support not going back to old ways. Simon suggested that developing a healthy routine would be very helpful in resisting triggers to drink, and he described the importance of making sure his new routine would not involve alcohol. I invited Jenna, his support person, to speak about the skills and values she had witnessed in Simon that he might draw on after his release to strengthen his commitment. Jenna described how she had witnessed Simon's impressive work ethic, his ability to build good relationships with those around him, and the unusual trust he had earned from the prison staff, all of which had contributed to him being a valued member of the unit.

I invited Simon to share his hopes for the future in line with this commitment, and he spoke of his wish to start a family, and of the possibility of doing educational talks to help others headed down a similar dangerous path.

Honouring legacy

Attending to the commitment to honour the loss of life, I asked Simon if he was open to hearing about who Gordon was and the kinds of things that were important to him during his life. When Simon agreed that he would be open to that, Josie had the opportunity to share how Gordon had been a person who was committed to social justice, how he left his estate to providing educational scholarships for disadvantaged young people and volunteered weekly at a soup kitchen. Without any input from me, Simon said that, while he knew he could never be a replacement for Gordon, the soup kitchen was close to his house and when he was released from prison he would be keen to undertake some volunteer shifts there. I asked Josie whether she thought Gordon would welcome this initiative, and Josie replied that Gordon most certainly would.

Creating space for expressions of regret, sorrow and remorse

A key concern was to ensure that experiences of regret or sadness could be spoken of, and I asked Simon if there were particular thoughts or sentiments that he wanted to let Josie know about. Simon relayed that he understood that an apology was not enough in these circumstances, but he did want Josie to understand that he was very sorry and cared very much about what he had done and the pain he had caused to people through his actions. Simon produced a letter of apology he had written to Josie, and spoke again of his sincere regret and remorse for causing Gordon's death.

Enabling contribution to each other and to social change

I had gone into this conference believing in possibilities for contribution to the lives of others as a consequence of this process, so I asked Josie what her hopes and wishes were for Simon's future. She said she didn't want two lives destroyed by this experience. When I asked if she thought Gordon might join with her in this hope, she reflected that Gordon would want Simon to have a fulfilling life, and to go on to make a positive contribution to the lives of others in the future. In response, Simon told Josie that it was important to him that she knew he was serious about his commitments and wondered if Josie would be open to future contact so that he could keep Josie up-to-date on how his commitments were going. He reflected that being in touch with her might also help him stay accountable to these commitments. Josie and Simon agreed that when Simon was released from prison, he and Josie would have contact every six or 12 months to talk about how Simon and his commitments were going.

During the conference, Josie learnt that Simon wasn't yet eligible for parole as he had not completed the required drug and alcohol programs.

He had been on a waiting list for years, but a backlog meant his name still hadn't come up. Josie was furious with the prison that Simon had been incarcerated for four years without receiving any services to address his struggles. After the conference, Josie wrote to the parole board to support Simon's application for parole.

Restorative conference as a powerful ritual

Rather than focusing solely on the restorative 'conference' in which Simon and Josie came together face-to-face, it is important to emphasise that this was a *process* that began from the very first interactions I had with the participants. The preparation process was crucial to providing the space to linger and build the foundations for the narrative themes of enabling contribution, thickening preferred storylines, honouring legacy and locating harm in wider structural contexts. This preparation enabled the conference to become a space of ritual in which preferred ways of being, identities and commitments could be made visible, with the other as an audience. I link this to the work of Barbara Myerhoff (1982), and to narrative therapy's use of definitional ceremony (White, 2007). Conference participants act as witnesses to one another. In this way, a restorative justice conference can operate as a powerful ritual for assisting people to redefine and reclaim their identities. The process can also provide public and community acknowledgment of preferred identity claims that stand in stark contrast to accounts, common in the criminal justice system, that are single-storied and often demonising of persons who have enacted harm.

After the conference

The restorative process did not end with the conference. Through phone calls I followed up with Simon and Josie about how they were feeling after the meeting. Simon relayed that he was glad he'd had the opportunity to talk to Josie. It was important to him that she knew he cared and didn't think of him as 'a piece of shit'. He said that knowing that Josie now knew that he cared helped him feel better about himself. Simon reflected that the conference had given him a voice and the chance to speak up, even if only a little. Simon said that meeting Josie had provided him with a face and stories to connect to Gordon, which he hadn't had access to previously.

Josie told me that she was pleased that she had met with Simon, and now had a better understanding about him and what had happened. She said she believed that Simon was willing to listen to her and take on what she had to say. She believed him to be genuine and not a bad person. Josie said that Simon's interest in Gordon and in learning from Gordon's ways was 'brilliant'. She recognised that Simon had a strong work ethic, which she thought, if channelled into good things, could make a difference.

In these phone calls I also clarified whether Simon and Josie were still willing to share their contact details with one another, in order that either party could make contact in the future. With their permission I sent them both the same letter documenting what had been talked about in the conference and some of the feedback captured during the follow-up phone calls. In this way, it was possible to create a counter document (White & Epston, 1990) that further thickened the preferred identity conclusions and commitments articulated during the conference. This letter recorded their preferred storylines and commitments, as witnessed by the other.

Further reflections: Sharing insights and learnings

I found myself wanting to better understand what had gone well in this conference. And, importantly, what could be shared with people in similar situations who were considering coming together to talk. I felt inspired to capture any reflections that might add to broader discussions about designing processes for accountability and responding to harm – ones not based on dominant discourses of punishment and retribution. In relation to his 'circle justice' work, Gatensky (1996) has reflected that the most powerful helpers are those 'who have gone through that very same process themselves ... they are the ones that can represent and speak from the heart' (1996, p. 199). Epston (1999) has argued that knowledges that are documented and compiled so they can be made available to others who are facing similar predicaments are 'fiercely and unashamedly pragmatic' (1999, p. 142).

So, a few months after the conference I sent Simon and Josie some questions about the skills and knowledge they had used during the process, and about the values that had supported their participation. I also asked what difference (if any) the conference had made. Both were happy to participate in this follow up, generously agreeing to their answers being made available to others, especially anyone considering taking part in a restorative justice conference. The following are extracts from their responses.

Renee: How did you know you were 'ready' to participate in a restorative justice conference?

Josie: For me, it was not really a question of being ready. I needed to know about the person who had caused the situation I was in and needed to hear what he had to say about it. Anything to shift the feeling of being a bystander in the justice process. I did not want to see myself as a victim; I wanted to regain some feeling of control over the situation – in a way that was more useful to me than the obvious response of anger and blame.

Simon: I just knew it was the right thing to do.

Renee: What kind of preparation did you do that you found helpful?

Josie: I talked to people who I thought would have some insight into the pros and cons of pursuing this. I visualised what it would be like to meet, what I would say and why. I thought about the fact that I might strongly dislike the person and that their response might be disappointing. I thought about what approach I could take to help make a meeting a positive experience. The exchange of information about our respective attitudes and feelings prior to the meeting helped me to prepare.

Renee: What was your goal or hope in participating?

Josie: To be engaged personally with the person rather than being an observer in an impersonal criminal justice system in which I had no control. For him to take responsibility for what happened and not make excuses. I didn't want to blame, belittle or refuse to listen to him. I hoped a consequent change in his behaviour/addiction/attitude would mean he would have a better life rather than worse life on release from prison. I also wanted to speak for my brother, so that it became more personal than Simon's role as a helpless player in the criminal justice system and mine as a victim.

Simon: To look Josie in the eyes and say sorry. I know that will never bring him back. I also wanted to show her that I'm learning from my stuff ups and once out of jail will stay on the right track.

Renee: What was most important to you in this process?

Josie: Honesty, mutual acknowledgment and understanding of the awful situation and the effect it had. The chance to have a conversation – listening, not just talking.

Simon: To talk to Josie face-to-face, to tell her that if there was anything she would like me to do for her brother I was down to do it. To tell her that I would never go back to being the old Simon.

Renee: What values/principles/beliefs did you draw on to guide your participation in this process?

Josie: The idea that change is possible. A person should not be imprisoned forever by their past. I could have an effect by the way I acted and should do that. I believe the social and criminal justice systems are flawed and was concerned that incarceration would reduce rather than increase his chance of a better life.

Renee: What were the parts of the process that felt the most scary, unknown or intimidating?

Josie: That moment of meeting for the first time. In my imagination this made me the most apprehensive.

Simon: The part that felt the most scary would have been that going into this, I did not know how I was going to be looked at. But the people involved made me feel safe in the room and I could open up then.

Renee: Was there anything that you were surprised by throughout this process?

Josie: I was surprised at how personally rewarding it was. He was frank, open and took responsibility. I felt able to give back, not through forgiveness but by letting him know that I had a stake in his future, which was a positive experience and I was surprised by how much I was willing to 'give' in this exchange. I was surprised that he felt deserving of a lengthy prison sentence and that he wasn't resentful and cynical about the lack of rehabilitation he had had in prison and that parole was still not on the agenda.

Simon: It surprised me how laid back it was. The biggest surprise would have been Josie. She made me feel like a person and did not talk down to me.

Renee: Did your view of the other person change during or after this process?

Josie: Yes. Most people have more courage than you expect. I left feeling hopeful for his future.

Simon: My view changed a lot because at first I really did think that the other family hated me. But as soon as I saw Josie she made me feel welcomed and let me open up a little. I thank Josie for that.

Renee: What kind of difference (if any) has participating in this process made to your life?

Josie: I have been able to deal with some of the feelings and experiences that followed the death of my brother, the investigation and the trial. It has made me conscious of the value of this restorative justice process and the pitiful ways in which our prison system fails offenders and society. It has encouraged me to do what I can to draw attention to this.

Renee: What would you want to share with someone else who was considering whether they wanted to participate?

Josie: It may be harder for others as I did not lose a child or my partner. I'd say try to be open minded and aware that it is a two-way process. 'Giving' to another person is actually very rewarding. Take the rare opportunity to talk and to listen to a person you would otherwise never meet, and who is critical to what you feel. Be brave and remember they probably have to be braver still. You have more to gain and less to lose by doing this than not, if you can manage it. There is no point participating if all you want to do is shout, belittle and blame the other person. There is no value in that for you.

Simon: All I would say to someone who wanted to take part in this is that at first you may feel the unknown about it all. Maybe you'll have 100 things going around in your head, but I can tell you that with all the people involved they make sure at all times

> you know what's going on and what will be asked. So there isn't anything from left field. They make sure you're happy with everything and you can stop at any time.

Simon and Josie's reflections highlight so many knowledges, learnings and insights that warrant further exploration.

My reflections on Josie and Simon's conference

I experienced Josie and Simon's restorative justice conference process as incredibly moving and encouraging. I witnessed the courage and generosity of spirit demonstrated by both parties in coming together, and the way they were able to sustain a respectful, honest and robust discussion.

I appreciated the way Josie was able to carry multi-storied hopes for the process and for Simon, and was able to express her desire to hold Simon accountable while simultaneously holding compassion, hope for his future and concern for his wellbeing. Fundamentally, her interactions with him were characterised by respect for Simon's humanity and dignity, despite the devastating harm his actions caused. I am interested in what made this stance possible for Josie, and in how this stance could be shared with others who have experienced harm. This might invite new understandings, or access forgotten or hidden desires for peace, that have potential to transform their own context of harm in powerful ways. I am interested in the effect this stance had on Simon and the subsequent conversation. I wonder what effect Josie's refusal to totalise Simon as the 'offender' have had on his ability to view himself differently. There is such a dominant social narrative that holding someone 'accountable' consists of making them feel bad about who they are and what they have done. It appears that Simon felt able to participate and share something of his life and that future accountability to commitments has been established through being treated with respect and dignity. I am interested in what these reflections can contribute to broader understandings of law and order, and to discourses of shame and punishment.

Of particular interest to me was Josie's desire to 'give' in this exchange. I'm also interested in the distinction she makes between her desire to 'give' and 'forgiveness'. I suspect this distinction might be important for others who have been harmed, who may feel the weight of the broader social narrative that the path to peace is to forgive. The concept of forgiveness is often devoid of notions of accountability and actions of repair. Josie positioning this 'giving' as having a stake in Simon's future strikes me as a powerful contribution to the possibility of transforming broader social conditions and contexts that have contributed to the occurrence of harm.

It has also been encouraging to see how this process enabled Simon to develop momentum for an alternative narrative of being 'someone who cares'; a counter story that stands in contrast to being a 'cold-hearted' person. Winslade and Monk (2000) suggested that we can think of this as a process of repositioning in relation to a dominant discourse. People can refuse the positions to which they are called and can establish their preferred positions as a response. These reflections also outline the significant development of multiple counter stories to the 'conflict story' between Simon and Josie. This collection of counter stories can be understood as a 'narrative of relationship' between the parties that is now incompatible with the stories associated with the original context of harm (Winslade & Monk, 2000, p. 4).

Following the conference, Josie sent me a song she had written and recorded, documenting some of her reflections and experience of the conference.

'Conviction Song' by Josie Walker

We met in the prison on a Monday morning
Neither of us knew how this would feel
He'd taken a life and I'd lost my brother
So a meeting like this just couldn't be real
They brought him in to where I sat waiting
Neither of us knew what we would say
He did not speak so I offered my hand
And the pain in his eyes looked back at me.

Do the crime do the time
make 'em all toe the line
And keep 'em locked away
Til the time is up, the time is up, the time.

He said you must be bitter you must be angry
Worthless kind of a man you think
You can shout you can swear for I am guilty
I killed your brother through drugs and drink
I've done four years and I want to promise you
I'll never do a thing like this again
But I can't help my 25 years of history
An honest promise might be in vain.

Do the crime do the time
make 'em all toe the line
And keep 'em locked away
Til the time is up, the time is up, the time.

I said no I'm not bitter, I'm not angry
That won't change what happened that night
But a promise to me must never be broken
I know now you can tell wrong from right
You've got to quit the drugs like you've had to quit drinking
Soon you'll be out and on parole
Parole means word and word means promise
It's a way we can make our two lives whole.

Do the crime do the time make 'em all toe the line
And keep 'em locked away
Til the time is up, the time is up, the time.

There's a big blank page that's called the future
A life where you fill the blank page in
Be a father raise your children
Or stay back where this begins
I'm reminded talking to you
That we are not worlds apart
Some bad choices lead to heartbreak
But the good ones give us heart.

Do the crime do the time make 'em all toe the line
And keep 'em locked away
Til the time is up, the time is up, the time.
Til the time is up, the time is up, the time.

Restorative process 2: the Hall and Dows families

On a long stretch of road in rural Australia, Tom's car crossed over on to Steven's side of the road and collided with Steven's car. That collision took the lives of two men, Tom and Steven. The coroner's report stated that Tom had suffered from severe mental illness for a large portion of his life and had expressed suicidal ideation in the days prior to the collision. Tom was unlicensed, had taken his mother's car without her knowledge and was not wearing a seat belt. The coroner concluded that suicide was a possibility, but she could not rule definitively on the cause of the collision due to Tom having an existing heart condition, exacerbated by the effects of long-term antipsychotic medication.

To Steven's family, the evidence provided pointed to suicide. They felt angry and upset at the coroner's findings, which left them with more questions than answers. They felt that Steven's life had been rendered 'invisible and worthless' through the process, and with no culpability assigned, or recommendations for future preventive actions, their feelings of 'injustice' compounded their immense sense of grief. Steven's mother was adamant that her son's death should not be for nothing. Steven's parents, Rosalie and John, reached out to investigate the possibility of having a restorative conference with Tom's family. Steven's parents were clear that they didn't blame Tom's family and meant them no harm, but they were devastated, angry and desperate for answers. In their minds, it was Tom's mental health that led to the death of their precious son. They hoped to honour Steven's legacy by contributing to change within the structures that had failed Tom. They wanted to know more about Tom and the circumstances and events that led up to the collision. Rosalie hoped there might be ways that both families could join together to advocate for improved care, and that some good might come from this tragedy.

Preparation

In thinking about bringing the two families together, I found myself considering a number of questions:

- How could we create a process for Steven's family that would give value and consideration to Steven's life? What difference would such a process make to their experience of 'injustice'?
- How could we create and enact such a process without burdening Tom's family with feelings of additional grief, blame and responsibility?
- How could we also honour the life of Tom and the suffering Tom and his family endured, alongside honouring the life of Steven?

Tom's mother, Rosalyn, and two sisters, Michelle and Elaine, agreed to meet with Steven's mother, Rosalie, father, John, and wife, Maggie.

During the prepatory conversations, Tom's mother said that she would never know what happened that day. She relayed how she wondered whether he might have looked down at the radio or perhaps he had a blackout. Although it broke her heart, she could accept that Tom may have made a decision to end his life by driving into a tree, but she could not accept, knowing the kind of person Tom was, that he decided to take his own life in a way that would also take the life of another. This sentiment was reiterated by Tom's sisters.

Both families demonstrated generosity and kindness in preparing to meet with the other, but this was fragile ground for both families. Preparatory conversations were key in firming up the ground beneath them. A key aspect of these preparatory conversations was working with both parties to define and agree on the purpose of coming together. Through multiple conversations with both families, everyone agreed on the following purposes for coming together:

- to help make sense of the loss through sharing information
- the possibility of creating some shared understandings
- to share grief, condolences and care
- for each family to honour and build on the legacies of Steven and Tom throughout the conversation

- to contribute to social and cultural change in the mental health system, or other advocacy.

The other crucial way of ensuring that both families could stand on more solid ground when they came together was inviting and celebrating preferred stories of Steven and Tom through the preparation process. This was made possible through questions drawn from re-membering practices (White, 2007):

- Catch me up on who Tom was. What was he like? Are there stories you can share with me that remind you of that quality?
- How will you keep this memory alive of Tom as you participate in this conversation? Who can help you with this?

Through tears, Tom's family relayed many stories about a kind, creative poet and photographer with a beautiful singing voice, who could sing the old South African anthem from memory. I asked similar questions of Steven's family, and Steven's mum and dad proceeded to tell me story after story, speaking over the top of each other, their faces lighting up as they remembered the kindness, positivity and brilliant mind of an engineer committed to sustainability. These conversations were crucial in making the process valuable for Steven's family. It was just as important that I did this for Tom's family, as they faced having lost their son and brother, and the possibility that he had acted intentionally, causing the death of someone else's son and brother. I needed to be sure that this process would allow Tom's family to continue to remember him in their preferred ways, and avoid making them feel responsible for Steven's death.

Part of the preparation was the careful process of introducing the families through sharing information and presenting each of the men who died in the collision to the other family. I worked with Steven's family to devise questions that were sent through to Tom's mother and sisters. My hope was that these questions would be gentle and accessible and elicit possibilities for discovering shared struggles, hopes and avenues for joining together. Through facilitating this exchange of questions and answers, I tested out opportunities for alternative meanings to be shaped, and for 'the diversity of available viewpoints' (Friedman, 1995, p. 224) to be made apparent. Winslade (2009) suggested that we can easily become separated and disconnected from our inner knowledges, desires for co-operation and hopes for living in peace when we stay in a single-storied version of the other and the way they have hurt us. For Steven's family, the understandable conclusion (due to a lack of conflicting evidence) that a faceless Tom had deliberately driven into their beloved son was an oppressive one. Learning alternative stories about Tom, his struggles, his hopes, his values and the reasons that Tom's mum was certain that this would not have been deliberate, could indeed be liberating for Steven's family.

Together, Steven's family and I constructed a series of questions, which Tom's mother and sister responded to in writing. I met with Steven's mother, father and wife to share the responses. I include here a few of the responses from Tom's mother.

How have you and your family been coping?

Rosalyn: Ups and downs, which I believe is normal. For me, a constant desperate sadness as I felt there was potential for a better chapter ahead for Tom, as he had just moved closer to home. Questions do not go away, same as the 'if only' thoughts. I have tried to keep busy, and take to my bed when it all gets too much.

The coroner's report only left us with more questions. How have you made sense of your son's and our son's deaths?

Rosalyn: I have not made sense, because of the questions; my thoughts are always 'perhaps this' or 'perhaps that'. I feel traumatised with the thought that Steven lost his life as a result; another family lost a loved one as well. I do not believe that Tom would have wanted or planned that. It was not in his nature.

Who was Tom and what was he like?

Rosalyn: Tom was an independent spirit, adventurous, had a good sense of humour, was intelligent, practical, caring and kind, loved the outdoors and cared about the environment.

What were his struggles?

Rosalyn: Mental health issues brought struggle into his life. Over 17 years he had periods where he fought desperately to manage his life again. He had periods when he was reasonably well and enjoyed different things, all the while having to deal with 'the system' and endure the horrible side effects of medication, which always plagued him.

Would you like to know more about Steven and his life? Who he was and what he was like?

Rosalyn: This is hard. I have thought of him as 'the other man' who lost his life in the collision, and that there is a family out there who have also lost a loved one and are going through what we are going through. I would like you to share something of him, even though I know it will be hard. I am going to meet his wife and his parents, and hear him talked about by name, and for me he will no longer be 'the other man'; he will be a very real person. This is hard. There are not many times when I think of Tom that I do not also think of Steven and his family.

Do you have any feelings or thoughts that we can make something positive come out of this?

Rosalyn: Being able to offer condolences, sympathy and care to you personally would be a positive for me.

Do you or your family have ideas about how the mental health system could have been improved to help your son and his family?

Rosalyn: This is a very big question, and a very complex one. Saying that, we have over time written to various ministers, complaints ombudsmen, hospitals etc.

As I read these responses to Steven's family their tears flowed, and the grief was palpable. There was a sense that these sentiments were longed for by Steven's family, especially Tom's mother expressing that whenever she thought of Tom, she also thought of Steven and his family. As I read this part aloud, I too wept with the family. Similarly, when I expressed Steven's family's sentiments to Tom's mother and sisters, particularly when they heard that Steven's family would like to know more about who Tom was and what his struggles were, there were tears of incredible grief – and perhaps of relief. They spoke of having wanted to send Steven's family a card at the time of the crash but not knowing how it would be received. At the time it felt too risky so they chose not to.

Restorative conference: Hall and Dows families come together

In the spirit of taking risks to create the conditions for possibilities, action and transformation, Steven's and Tom's families came together in a meeting room attached to a local library in rural Australia.

Conscious of the increased levels of anxiety the participants might experience in meeting for the first time, I spent time creating physical reminders in the room to orientate participants to the purpose and principles of the meeting. I placed chairs in a circle. In the middle of the circle of chairs I placed circles of paper, capturing the shared purposes of our coming together. In among these I placed another set of circles capturing some of the principles each participant had suggested were important to them in this conversation. And with the participants' prior consent, I also added principles I had witnessed them display towards one another in preparing for this meeting.

The collective guiding principles were:

- generosity (acknowledging the generosity of each participant in agreeing to meet)
- kindness (show care and compassion to each participant)
- curiosity (openness to new learnings and understandings)
- patience (for the time it takes to build trust and relationships)
- respect for diversity (of opinions, ways of grieving, understandings, future hopes).

Both families' capacity for kindness and generosity was expressed as the participants entered the room, met each other in person for the first time and immediately embraced. I invited them to join me in the circle and began by acknowledging their generosity, courage and the deep respect I had for each participant in agreeing to take part. I shared that I was continually inspired by my conversations with each one of them, and that witnessing what these two families had agreed to do in coming together sparked courage in my own life to do things that were difficult and painful. I intentionally chose to start the conversation by offering something to the group to build good will among participants and help to solidify the ground from which we would traverse to more difficult or painful topics. I had gathered quotes from my preparation meetings with the participants that spoke to the intentions and hopes they carried into the meeting. I shared them with the group as a way of introducing the participants to each other. These quotes offered sympathy and condolences to one another. They spoke of shared grief, confusion and of thinking of the other family. They told of knowing this would be a difficult and stressful process but hoping that understandings could be arrived and that everyone would find something positive in the process.

I then invited the families to share something with each other about how they had been coping and/or responding to losing Tom and Steven.

The conversation between the two families flowed from this point. As a facilitator, I chose to say very little, just guiding the conversation on a few occasions. I had a strong feeling that my role was primarily in the preparation work of building trust and connection between the two families prior to them coming together, and the more the conversation could flow between the two families without my help, the better.

The following is a summary of the conversation captured under themes that were discussed.

Sharing grief, condolences and care

The Dows family talked about the pain of losing Steven, and the Hall family of the pain of losing Tom. Both families also spoke of recognition of one another's suffering, their shared experience and the regret that any of them had to go through this at all.

Throughout the meeting, stories of the strategies they used for managing the grief emerged. Much of the support that had been offered by others had gradually drifted away, leaving expectations that they should move on. Rosalyn felt she was on 'autopilot' some days. Rosalie commented that it was like trying to make sense of something that didn't make sense. They acknowledged the different ways people cope and how sometimes it felt hard to find purpose again. Elaine spoke about organising an exhibition of Tom's photos to express her pride in him and his creative talents. Both families spoke of how the other family had often been in their thoughts since the collision.

Tom and his family's journey with the mental health system

The Hall family relayed some of Tom's 17-year history with the mental health system, during which he had 23 inpatient admissions, some of up to three months. They spoke of a system that had failed to respond to Tom as an individual person who needed care, and focused on medicating people. Frequent staff turnover, with some not suited to working with vulnerable people, meant that Tom could not establish a relationship of continuity with the people treating him. The Halls saw this as an important factor in Tom losing trust in those responsible for his treatment. The psychiatrist only met with Tom once or twice a year and, despite Rosalyn's repeated requests, never agreed to meet with her. It was this psychiatrist who had changed Tom's medication, marking the beginning of a particularly hard time for Tom and his family, without assistance with the withdrawal process.

A case manager visited to administer Tom's medication daily at 2pm, completely wiping him out for the second half of every day, which he hated. But the mental health service said they could not accommodate a different schedule. The case manager would go through a checklist of questions with Tom, asking him 'are you suicidal?' in a very routine way and there was no sense they were genuinely interested in how Tom was doing. This contributed to Tom's disengagement. The Hall family talked about how the mental health system's failure to include the family in Tom's treatment meant they experienced years of frustration and feeling 'kept in the dark' by a system that limited their ability to help Tom to their fullest capacity, leaving Rosalyn feeling useless and helpless. Rosalyn spoke of the need to focus on improving people's quality of life and nurturing the person, something Tom did not receive from those responsible for his treatment.

How things were for Tom leading up to the crash

The Halls told how Tom had lived in public housing that was ridden with mice, horrible and unsafe. Tom worried about his safety and kept his security door locked at all times. The general environment was so depressing that to get Tom away from this awful living situation, Michelle and Elaine had bought him a flat in a town close to Rosalyn. The Hall family had all helped Tom move and he was very happy about his new place, giving the family hope that this would be the start of a new, brighter chapter for Tom. However, things continued to be hard and his medication was not working for him. The Halls think he was very depressed, overwhelmed and couldn't see a way out. Tom desperately wanted a job, something meaningful to do, and his physical health was poor. Rosalyn told of how the Friday before the crash she met with Tom's case manager, and told her Tom was scared to walk to the supermarket in case he collapsed. Rosalyn believed something was going on with Tom's physical health.

Rosalie and John also talked about the coroner's report, stating that in the days before the crash, Tom had told his case manager that he no longer wanted to live. They wanted to know how this was responded to by those treating Tom, commenting that such a statement means the person needs help and care. The Halls didn't know what steps the mental health service had taken in response to Tom's statement and also felt let down by the coronial process that failed to investigate the mental health service's actions.

Maggie asked the Halls if they knew where Tom was going on the day of the crash, but they didn't know. Tom hadn't driven in years, and Rosalyn wondered if Tom had a plan to drive into tree or a dam, but she did not believe he would have planned to drive into another person. Nor could she discount cardiac arrhythmia as a possible explanation.

Advocacy for mental health system change

The Halls made complaints both before and after Tom died, but found multiple barriers. Rosalie and John also felt committed to advocating for change within the mental health system to prevent others from experiencing something similar. Each family member talked about taking steps towards advocating for change, arguing that help should aim to avert a crisis not wait until someone is in a crisis before intervening. They spoke of people needing support, care and nurturing, and of families needing to be kept informed and included. They acknowledged the need for a societal response to mental health.

Honouring Steven's legacy

Rosalie and John said Steven was 'delightful' as a child with the 'gift of the gab', always making, inventing and experimenting. Steven and his sister each had a calf when they were children and Steven suggested making methane gas out of cow poo and a tin can, successfully carrying out this project. Once he towed home 200 metres of poly pipe on his motorbike to make a wind turbine, and had been very interested in renewable energy throughout his life. He'd say to John, 'I want to make a hydrogen generator. Let's go down to the shed'. John shared very happy memories of working on projects with Steven, and said that he still had conversations with Steven when he was working in the shed. Steven was a 'people person' who 'made fun wherever he went' and 'lit up the room'. Maggie said, 'Steven was a wonderful man. It took me a long time to find him. He ticked all the right boxes. I miss him'.

Honouring Tom's legacy

Before he became unwell, Tom was athletic and active. He was interested in technology and design. After finishing high school, he went backpacking around the world for 10 or 11 months with Michelle and Elaine. Tom's family described him as kind and gentle, unable to walk past someone without offering to help. He would help old ladies in the supermarket, and engage with the person at the supermarket checkout to get them laughing. When he lived in Melbourne, even though it was a hard time, Tom had friends. People at the local op shop and cafes knew him and were kind to him. Tom knew how to connect with people, and Elaine described him as a 'big merry guy with lots of wild hair'. Tom took beautiful photographs and wrote poetry.

Towards the end of the conference, one of Tom's poems was read out to the group.

I've caught a dusting of sunshine,
a starfish, teasing butterflies
tender kisses:
a pocketful of dreams

Then woven these threads of silver and gold,
coloured with laughter, a wink
gentle warmth:
a cloth of rays that gleams

As full as any picnic basket
packed up tightly with fond memories
for when you're sad
or not as bold

When on unfolding,
spreading all around, igniting your soul
from deepest blue
to brightest gold

In a compassionate and tender gesture, Steven's mother asked if she could take a copy of Tom's poem home with her.

After three long and emotional hours of questions, sharing, tears and occasional laughter, all participants agreed that they were happy to draw the conversation to a close.

Post-conference reflections

In follow up conversations, Rosalie and John shared some moving and important reflections about what they had learnt about Tom, which highlighted the multiple and varied stories they now carried of the person they believed to be responsible for their son's death. They now understood more of his life and struggles, and the systems that were against him. They also offered post-conference reflections about the importance of having found ways to honour both men through this process, and how this gave Rosalie and John a sense that their son's life was of some consequence. They reflected that honouring Steven's life in this way was in direct contrast to the lack of justice they experienced interacting with an impersonal Coroner's Court.

Following this process, both families agreed to stay in touch, and to find ways to collaborate in broader advocacy in response to the failings of the mental health system.

Conclusion

As I reflect on the ongoing isolation and the dominant, all-encompassing narratives that each of these participants was carrying before the opportunity to come together to share their experiences, concerns, pain and hopes from an experience of harm and loss, I feel as though I have been given such a precious opportunity. I feel privileged in having had the opportunity to interrupt the dominant meanings and narratives that those involved in these conferences had previously cemented, not only as a consequence of the profound losses they experienced, but due to the destructive mechanisms of the criminal justice system that encouraged conflict, and failed to address their needs for or understandings of justice, healing, information, connection or peace.

Both of these restorative processes suggest to me that rich story development and uncovering the resonances found in sharing stories, commitments and purposes can transform identities, beliefs and stances. These experiences also suggest that capacity for safety, accountability, social change and healing from harms can be found in acknowledging our collective humanity and having the courage to travel together to places where harms can be addressed – and sometimes even harnessed for future transformation of individual and social conditions. I feel invigorated when I see the possibilities created by this work. In these moments I get a feeling that the world I want to see is possible; that human beings are capable of the kind of reflection, strength, spirit, generosity and wisdom that will ensure we are all going to be okay. Maybe even better than okay.

Postscript

Since this chapter was first written, Simon has been released from prison. Since his release, Simon and Josie have had a long phone conversation and agreed to keep in contact. Rosalie and Rosalyn collaborated on a joint submission to the Royal Commission into Victoria's Mental Health System and advocated to VicRoads for improved safety provisions at the scene of the collision. They remain in contact and have met on various occasions for coffee and lunch.

Acknowledgments

I would like to express particular appreciation and gratitude for David Denborough, David Newman, Rachel Herzing and Nareeda Lewers for assisting me to navigate and reflect on these processes. In moments of doubt, each of you played a role in helping shape my next steps through sharing your wisdom, ideas and reflections. A final thank-you to Kristina Lainson who was patient and generous with her time in helping to shape this chapter.

Notes

[1] Creative Interventions is a grassroots organisation in California, USA, that seeks creative and collective responses to end interpersonal violence. For more information see: http://www.creative-interventions.org

[2] Generation Five is a small volunteer organisation in the USA, dedicated to the eradication of childhood sexual abuse without relying on police or prisons. For more information see http://www.generationfive.org

References

Creative Interventions. (2018). *StoryTelling and organizing project.* Retrieved from www.stopviolenceeveryday.org

Denborough, D. (1996). *Beyond the prison: Gathering dreams of freedom.* Adelaide, Australia: Dulwich Centre Publications.

Denborough, D. (2008). *Collective narrative practice: Responding to individuals, groups, and communities who have experienced trauma.* Adelaide, Australia: Dulwich Centre Publications.

Denborough, D. (2011). *Collective narrative practice: Eliciting and richly describing local skills and knowledges in communities responding to hardship* (PhD Thesis). La Trobe University, Melbourne, Australia.

Dixon, E., & Piepzna-Samarasinha, L. (2020). Beyond survival: Strategies and stories from the transformative justice movement. Chico, CA: AK.

Epston, D. (1999). Co-research: The making of an alternative knowledge. In *Narrative therapy and Community Work: A conference collection* (pp. 137–157). Adelaide, Australia: Dulwich Centre Publications.

Friedman, S. (1995). *The reflecting team in action.* New York, NY: Guilford.

Gatensky, H. (1996). Circle Justice. In D Denborough (Ed.), *Beyond the prison: Gathering dreams of freedom.* (pp. 181–199) Adelaide, Australia: Dulwich Centre Publications.

Generation Five. (2018). *Ending child sexual abuse: A transformative justice handbook.* Retrieved from http://www.generationfive.org/wp-content/uploads/2017/06/Transformative-Justice-Handbook.pdf

Kim, M. (2018). From carceral feminism to transformative justice: Women-of-color feminism and alternatives to incarceration. *Journal of Ethnic and Cultural Diversity in Social Work, 27*(3), 219–233.

Mitchell, S. (2006). Debriefing after traumatic situations – using narrative ideas in the Gaza Strip. In D. Denborough (Ed.), *Trauma: Narrative responses to traumatic experience* (pp. 103–113). Adelaide, Australia: Dulwich Centre Publications.

Morgan, A. (2000). *What is narrative therapy? An easy-to-read introduction.* Adelaide, Australia: Dulwich Centre Publications.

Myerhoff, B. (1982). Life history among the elderly: Performance, visibility, and remembering. In J. Ruby (Ed.), *A crack in the mirror: Reflexive perspectives in anthropology* (pp. 99–117). Philadelphia: University of Pennsylvania Press.

Ostaseski, F. (2017). *The five invitations: Discovering what death can teach us about living fully.* London, England: Pan Macmillan.

Schulman, S. (2016). *Conflict is not abuse.* Vancouver, Canada: Arsenal.

Welch, S. (1990). *A feminist ethic of risk.* Minneapolis, MN: Fortress.

White, M. (2000). Re-engaging with history: The absent but implicit. In M. White (Ed.), *Reflections on narrative practice* (pp. 35–58). Adelaide, Australia: Dulwich Centre Publications.

White, M. (2007). *Maps of narrative practice.* New York, NY: Norton.

White, M., & Epston, D. (1990). *Narrative means to therapeutic ends.* New York, NY: Norton.

Winslade, J. (2009). The secret knowledge of peacemaking. *Negotiation Journal, 25*(4), 559–568.

Winslade, J., & Monk, G. (2000). *Narrative mediation*. San Francisco, CA: Jossey-Bass.

Winterson, J. (2001, October 3). We are all frightened. There is no safety without risk. What you risk reveals what you value. *The Guardian*. Retrieved from www.theguardian.com/world/2001/oct/02/gender.uk1

Zehr, H. (2002). *The little book of restorative justice*. Intercourse, PA: Good Books.

About the authors

Sekneh Hammoud-Beckett is a registered psychologist and narrative therapist. She currently works in private practice providing therapy, teaching and supervision. When not immersed in the therapeutic space, Sekneh is engaged in community advocacy roles.

Tileah Drahm-Butler is an Aboriginal woman of the Darumbal/Kulilli and Wanyurr Majay Yidinji Nations of Queensland, Australia and lives in Cairns, North Queensland. Tileah is a social worker with a Master of Narrative Therapy and Community Work. Tileah works in the emergency department of a busy regional hospital and is on the Dulwich Centre International Teaching Faculty where she leads the teaching of narrative therapy and community work through an Aboriginal lens in Australia and internationally. Tileah has also been appointed as Co-chair of Feminisms, Intersectionality and Narrative Practice at Dulwich Centre. Tileah can be contacted at: tileahdb@dulwichcentre.com.au

Jill Faulkner comes from Aotearoa (NZ); however, she has lived more of her life on Aboriginal lands than on her own grandfather's country. She has worked with children, families and communities for more than 30 years. Jill's thinking and work are shaped by the multiple relationships and storied journeys that she has travelled alongside these folks. Jill is a grassroots worker committed to supporting space for people to engage in healing of past hurts and to work for systemic and structural reform. Jill can be contacted at: faulkner.jill@gmail.com

Alyssha Mary Fooks is a practitioner based in Melbourne, Australia. With over 15 years' experience working in the health and community sectors, she has worked alongside individuals and communities and been involved in numerous research and community projects, including policy development and advocacy. The focus of Alyssha's work has been on preventing and responding to violence and harm, including working to challenge racism and attend to privilege in the health and community sector. She seeks to move towards justice and addressing health inequalities. Alyssha can be contacted at: alyssha.fooks@gmail.com

Renee Handsaker works as a facilitator specialising in responding to harm between people and groups. Renee also works across a number of institutions to facilitate restorative responses to historical abuse. Renee is currently employed with Open Circle, a restorative justice service connected to the Centre for Innovative Justice in Melbourne, Victoria. Renee can be contacted at: renee.handsaker@rmit.edu.au

Simangaliso Brenda Nyoni has 11 years' experience as a social worker and counsellor. She is currently employed as a counsellor at Deakin University. Simangaliso completed a Bachelor of Social Work and Master of Counselling, both at Latrobe University. She started this journey as an international student from Zimbabwe with the aim of becoming a counsellor to support women and children who have experienced all forms of violence. She has worked with asylum seekers, people who have experienced homelessness, in child protection services and as a sexual assault counsellor-advocate. She always comes from a place of enquiry and curiosity when she is providing counselling support and aims to provide a safe space for people to share their experiences without judgement. Simangaliso can be contacted at: brendasimanga84@gmail.com